QUIET THE ITTY BITTY SHITTY COMMITTEE

A guide to remembering all that you are

Five Self-Love Tools to Silence Your Inner Critic and Reclaim Your Worth

AUDREY SUTTON MILLS

For the woman who felt the quiet pull to open this book,
the one remembering her spark, her voice, her truth.

May you trust what is rising within you
and claim your freest, fullest expression.

And for my dad,
who believed in me every step of the way.
I feel you still.

Dear beautiful one,

If this book has found its way into your hands, I don't believe it's random. I believe in synchronicity. I believe in divine timing. And I believe something in your heart is calling you here.

Maybe you're standing at a threshold where the old ways no longer fit, but the new hasn't fully revealed itself. Maybe you're craving more—more ease, more freedom, more meaning, more you. Or perhaps you're sensing that who you've been is no longer who you're becoming, and something deeper within you is ready to be lived.

I want you to know, **I see you.**

I see your strength, your tenderness, your resilience, and your longing. And I also know this to be true. *You are already worthy.*

You don't have to prove it. You don't have to earn it.

You never did. Worth is your birthright.

Over time, we take on stories that were never ours to carry: rules about who we should be, how much we should do, or how small we need to stay to belong. The inner critic grows louder, and we begin to doubt our intuition and dim parts of ourselves.

The five self-love tools in this book help you quiet the *Itty Bitty Shitty Committee* and its limiting beliefs and self-sabotaging patterns, so you can see your true self: ever-expansive, creative, loving, and abundant.

This book is here to help you remember *all* that you are.

As you move through these pages, my hope is that you feel supported in your healing, grounded in presence, and guided back to your inner wisdom. That little by little, the inner critic falls away and what remains is the truth of who you are beneath the conditioning, the fear, and the striving.

You are already whole.

You are already enough.

This is a journey of sacred remembrance. A reclamation of your worth. A return to your truest, freest, most sovereign self. The one who has been here all along, quietly waiting for you to come home.

I'm so honored to walk beside you.

With love,
Audrey

TABLE OF CONTENTS

YOU ARE NOT ALONE

It was New Year's Eve and my 31st birthday. I was hammered. It was supposed to be my dream celebration, with twenty-two of our closest friends gathered with us at Garfinkel's, a popular dance bar in Whistler, Canada. My friends were having a blast dancing under the neon lights, drinking and laughing in our VIP booths. Sweaty champagne glasses clinked to ring in the new year and my birthday. As the DJ counted down, "Five, four, three, two . . ." a truth I'd been trying to bury surged up in my chest. I couldn't swallow it anymore. I turned to my husband and shouted, "I want a divorce!"

If this were a movie, the DJ's record would screech to a halt, and everyone would turn wide-eyed to stare at me. But time didn't stand still. Only I did.

From the outside, I looked like I had a charmed life. By twenty-five, I was one of Silicon Valley's top real estate agents, already making multiple six figures. From my two-bedroom home, I built a luxury real-estate company that grew to eight offices and more than a hundred agents. I owned a beautiful Spanish bungalow, had awesome friends, took spectacular vacations, and married a handsome, successful, really good man.

How could I check off all the boxes for my dream life but still feel utterly empty? Maybe you've had a moment like that too, when everything looks fine on the outside, but something inside you quietly whispers: *This isn't it.*

What people didn't see was that I was overworked, overstressed, and on a hamster wheel I didn't know how to get off. Always striving and striving, and never resting. My self-worth lived in what I achieved instead of who I was. Eight to ten times a week, I numbed out with fast food and anesthetized myself with caffeine, alcohol, and Ambien, to name a few. My hair was falling out in clumps, my joints aching, my body wildly waving red flags, but I was too busy sprinting on life's treadmill to slow down, tune in, and heed them.

As Oprah has often shared, life whispers to us first. When we ignore those whispers, the message gets louder: a thump upside the head, then a brick, until eventually the whole wall comes crashing down and we're forced to listen.

I can't count the number of times I'd been blackout drunk the year leading up to that New Year's Eve breakdown. One morning still stands out. I woke with my head pounding as though a little gremlin lived behind each eyeball, drumming to the beat of my heart. My body ached as if I'd been to a boxing class instead of happy hour. I was sprawled across the couch. One black Manolo stiletto dangling from my toes, the other foot stuck to the floor.

Evidence was scattered across the coffee table: greasy fingerprints and a fast-food bag ripped down the center like a javelina had devoured it. Apparently, at 3:00 a.m., I'd gone all in. A patty melt, curly fries, and even a sausage croissant breakfast meal. *Wow. Two meals? Really?*

I pulled a clip-on hair extension from my rat's nest of hair and set it alongside the other pieces of evidence. In the bathroom, I found my underwear and another hair extension on the floor. Playing detective, I followed the trail: my other shoe was by the back door, my keys outside on the step, and my Mercedes sat in the driveway with my strapless sticky bra clinging to the windshield. *Classy! Get it together.*

It was 6:32 a.m. My husband had already left for his San Francisco commute. When he walked by my fast-food crime scene and my lifeless body, he probably clicked his tongue in disgust before locking the front door behind him. He didn't even wake me. No nudge. No boot on my shoulder. That's just the kind of guy he was, composed and considerate.

I was unconsciously acting out, like a naughty child throwing tantrums and expecting someone to notice. Deep down, I hoped he would yank me out of the tornado I kept spinning in. My behavior was a cry for help.

My husband never said a thing about my behavior or who I was with. In fact, we never talked about anything uncomfortable. We danced around each other, careful not to stir conflict. We swept emotions under the rug and hoped the mess would disappear.

But of course, it never did.

What you avoid always finds you. First it knocks. If you still don't answer, it breaks down the door and slaps your bra on the windshield for the neighbors to see.

I picked up a cold, half-eaten hash brown, dipped it into the clotted ketchup, and shoved it in my mouth. I wasn't ready to deal with it yet, but life was. Sometimes life has to break us open so we can finally hear our own heart trying to break free.

That New Year's Eve on the dance floor, I broke wide open. The only way back to wholeness was to repair my fragmented pieces.

Poet Mark Nepo writes, "We either willfully shed or we are broken open."

Our breakdowns often lead to our biggest breakthroughs. So, I went on a decade-long journey to heal and find myself. This book is my heart and soul, everything I've learned from others and from experience.

What I discovered is that no amount of *external* success can fill an *internal* void. If you don't feel good enough *before* you get the things you think will make you happy—the relationship, the money, the achievements—you won't feel good enough *after*.

Ironically, my search to "find myself" showed me it was never about finding anything at all. You don't track your worth down like a misplaced stiletto.

Our soul's journey is to unlearn who you were taught to be, and remember who you truly are. It's the reclamation of your truest, freest, most sovereign self, the one who has been here all along, waiting for you to come home.

Over the past decade, I've not only used these tools in my own life but taught them to hundreds of clients. They've helped heal unworthiness, embrace the parts we've hidden in shame, and learn to trust and love ourselves *fully*.

> *No amount of external success can fill an internal void.*

These self-love tools carried me through divorce, the loss of my dad, big career pivots, miscarriage, and a dark postpartum season. They helped me stop abandoning myself and finally stand in my own corner—whole, free, and sovereign.

This is the book I wish I had ten years ago. So I wrote it for you. Because if you're here, maybe you've been wishing for it too.

As you move through this book, each chapter will meet you where you are. I'll begin with stories from my own life, moments of breakdown, awakening, and remembering, before guiding you into a simple self-love tool you can apply in your own life. Each chapter closes with a practice, reflection questions, and an exploration of how this work connects to your energy body through the chakras.

My invitation is to move slowly, listen inward, and let this be something you practice and live, not something you rush through. Think of this book as a guide you can return to again and again, a companion on the path to remembering who you truly are and aligning with your worthy and sovereign self. The tools inside aren't meant to be understood only once. They are meant to be practiced, revisited, and lived as you continue unfolding into your truest self.

And chances are, you picked up this book for a reason. Something inside you knows it's time.

Do you ever feel stuck in a loop of self-doubt, questioning if you're enough? When the self-judgment is so harsh it stifles your dreams? I've been where you are. And maybe that's why you picked up this book. Because you, too, have an inner critic. Mine isn't just one voice. It's a whole committee! That relentless inner dialogue that doubts, judges, and sabotages you.

But fighting or silencing it only makes it stronger. Instead, you'll learn to befriend your Itty Bitty Shitty Committee. *Wait, what?* Yep, uh-huh. Because the truth is, you can't get rid of your inner critic, but you can understand its fears and its shame, and stop letting it run the show.

> *Our soul's journey is to remove the false layers that cover who we are, so we can remember all that we are.*

When you stop doubting yourself and start loving your whole self, you'll not only trust yourself, you'll trust life too.

Does that mean the inner critic goes away forever? Heck no! We're human. We still get triggered, fall into old patterns, and feel messy emotions. I'm right there with you. I'm not a therapist; I'm a self-love guide. And I'm human, just like you, walking this path alongside you.

Life isn't about erasing the messy parts; it's about meeting them with compassion. Our soul's journey is to remove the false layers that cover who we are, so we can remember *all* that we are.

I wrote this book to help you come home to the part of you that already knows she's worthy. When you embrace *all* of yourself, the dark and the light, you unlock a trust so deep you stop searching outside for happiness. The love, worthiness, abundance is already within you.

Somewhere along the way, we forget. From the moment we're born, we absorb messages: *Be happy. Be good. Don't be too much.* We mold ourselves to fit in and silence parts of who we are just to feel loved and connected.

I often picture it like this: We are born into a magnificent castle with endless rooms representing the myriad parts of our personality, each one holding our creativity, joy, wildness, and quirks.

As children, we wander freely through every room, opening each door with curiosity and delight, simply exploring the fullness of who we are.

But as we grow, people enter our castle and start judging: *This room is too much. That one's too messy. That one's too loud. That one's too wild. Don't show that part of yourself. People might not like it.* Slowly, we begin closing doors within ourselves, shutting off parts of our most authentic self.

Then we visit other people's castles, comparing our rooms to theirs.

More doors close.

One by one, we close off the rooms of our beautiful castle that once felt alive with possibility and freedom. Door by door, we shut away parts of ourselves that don't quite fit the expectations of the world around us.

Before long, we're living in a one-bedroom fixer-upper, wondering why we feel so disconnected.

This book is your key back in.

I call these self-love tools the **5 C's: Consciousness, Care, Compassion, Curiosity, and Connection.** Together, they form the foundation of self-love and the path to your sacred remembrance. These five practices brought me back home to my worth. And now, I want to share them with you.

Every challenge and every relationship is an invitation: open a door back to your true self, or keep it shut. Expand into who you are, or shrink into who you were told to be.

Because here's what I know: self-love isn't a feel-good idea. It's the foundation for everything. When you reclaim your worth, you stop chasing validation and start trusting your own heart.

So, are you ready to open the doors and explore your whole, vibrant self? To quiet the Itty Bitty Shitty Committee and follow the whispers of your heart?

You don't have to know how. It begins the moment you're willing to remember yourself.

Let's begin.

CHAPTER 1

THE ITTY BITTY SHITTY COMMITTEE

"When you ghost your own greatness, you risk doubting yourself out of your destiny."

– JAMIE KERN LIMA

Okay, this was rock bottom. Run-down and on the brink of a melt-down in my early thirties, I found myself in a 'gentle yoga' class, doing seated floor poses with five 80-year-old men, wondering how I got here.

During Savasana, a supine resting pose, the yoga instructor guided us through a meditation. We silently counted our breath: inhale (one), exhale (two), inhale (three), exhale (four), and so forth. Whenever we noticed a thought pop into our mind, we would start over and begin counting again at one. It seemed easy enough.

I couldn't get past two. TWO!

Asking me to simply "watch your thoughts" was like asking me to recite *The Odyssey* in Latin. *If I'm not my thoughts, then who am I?* I'd need a second cappuccino just to figure that one out.

So, I breathed and tried to be still. But the harder I tried to breathe calmly, the harder it was to breathe. My leg began to twitch. My foot went numb. Then came the parade of distractions: an ache in my back, an itch on my cheek, my jaw locking, nervous sweat pooling under my arms. I needed to move. The silence was deafening!

Whenever I tried to control a thought and make it go away by thinking of something else or ignoring it, the thought only got louder. It felt like my body was straight-up allergic to meditation.

Breathe in. Breathe out.

After a few minutes of deep breathing, my body began to relax, and I began sinking into the dark chasm of my mind. Muffled, murmured voices lurked there. I strained to eavesdrop on the jumbled commotion of voices, each with its own personality and dialogue. I tried to stay afloat and listen to the voices one at a time, but they all weighed me down and made me feel like I was drowning.

Where the heck did these voices come from? How could I have lived with these voices for decades without knowing they were there?

It was like a clown car in my head...one voice after another piling out, ranting and judging. I wanted to scream SHUT UP! but remembered I was in a dang yoga class, and no one was yelling at me.

Hey, crazy lady! I'm the one yelling! In. My. Head.

Forget the geriatric yoga class, *this* was rock bottom. Clearly, I'd lost my damn mind. I quickly brushed one tear from my cheek and another, but the tears were spilling out too fast. Something in me had ruptured like a dam. It was my heart. It broke open. And now my sadness, shame, insecurities, and unworthiness were flooding out. I was unraveling fast.

There's a saying: "If you don't want to change, don't do yoga." This is why I'd avoided stepping into those hippy, woo-woo, free-thinking yoga rooms. On an elliptical machine, I didn't have to be with my thoughts. In twenty minutes, I could break a sweat while scrolling on my phone and drinking a soda.

But here on my yoga mat, I couldn't check out or distract myself. There was nowhere to run. So I forced myself to stay with the voices in my head to see where they would lead me. I'd been running all my life, and clearly, I wasn't getting anywhere.

So, I tried to concentrate on breathing deeply to slow the spinning sensation I felt. *Inhale. Exhale.* My mind was like a knotted necklace. The more I tried to untangle the voices, the more gnarled they became. *Breathe. Let go. Be here.*

After a few minutes of deep breathing and gentle attention, I began to disentangle the voices. I could hear the individual dialogues. I listened and observed. It was like hosting an endless panel of characters—nagging, gossiping, judging—all feasting on my soul one nitpicking bite at a time. Each character replayed its persistent storyline: the victim, the persecutor, the procrastinator, the drill sergeant, the insecure girl, the jealous girl, the angry girl, the unworthy girl, the fearful girl, the show-off, the worrier, the phony.

I so badly wanted to slink out of that prison disguised as a yoga studio and speed through the nearest drive-thru so I could stuff my feelings into some creamy Chick-fil-A sauce and feel something different. Anything to escape the torment of these mental gangsters.

Although this was the first time I paid attention to these voices, they were familiar. If I was really honest with myself, they'd been there for as long as I could remember, lurking in the shadows, a hushed rumbling like freeway noise, constantly reminding me I was never good enough.

Throughout the suffocating noise, I latched on to my breath, riding each steady inhalation and exhalation to ventilate my heart. Between each thought, each voice, each character, there was a tiny gap of relief. Minuscule, but enough to rest my busy mind into the heart. The slower I breathed and witnessed the voices without abandoning them, the more tender spaces opened up. Slowly, the orphaned thoughts and voices found a home. One by one, the rants were quieted, the voices lulled, and my breathing steadied.

The edginess in my mind softened, and there was subtle space. My body buzzed, relieved and exhausted. It was like I'd just gulped two handfuls of shrooms and strapped into a mental rollercoaster. Returning to my body now, I realized I was still lying on the floor of a yoga class.

While I'd been at the circus funhouse in my head, everyone else had been lying peacefully in Savasana.

What the heck just happened? If I can watch my thoughts, then I'm not in them. And if I'm not my thoughts, maybe I don't have to let them run my life.

The realization both intrigued and unnerved me. For the first time, I sensed someone else inside me—*me*, but bigger. Not my body, not my stories, not this woman in the middle of a divorce lying on a yoga floor.

> *If I can watch my thoughts, then I'm not in them. And if I'm not my thoughts, maybe I don't have to let them run my life.*

Just...me. The *real* me.

And in that moment, I felt a tiny spark of freedom.

Class was over, but I lingered on my mat, lying there with my eyes still closed until I heard the last yogi shuffle out of the room. When I got up, I saw the yoga teacher looking at me, her blue eyes piercing my soul. *Yikes! How long had she been in the corner watching me?* Embarrassed, I quickly wiped my tear-stained face, feigned a crooked smile, and stammered an apology for staying too long.

The teacher, an all-knowing, blonde Buddha, put her hand on my shoulder. After a long, awkward pause, she said, "You're ready." Her kind eyes twinkled, and she glided out of the room without saying another word.

Yoga people are so weird!

I didn't know it then, but that was the beginning of my transformation. That was the beginning of discovering that I'd been listening to the wrong voices.

Our Inner Saboteur

Everyone has an inner saboteur, that negative voice that drags us down the scarcity elevator, convincing us we're not good enough and don't have enough. Maybe you're like me and don't have just one voice but a whole committee of attackers. That yoga class was my first conscious encounter with the voices that had been bullying me for decades. I call them the Itty Bitty Shitty Committee. This pessimistic crew will say the meanest things to convince us we'll never be enough.

The Itty Bitty Shitty Committee replays the highlight reel of our failures, every "should," every "not enough," looping like a broken record. When the Committee runs the show, our perspective shrinks, our walls go up, and our hearts close down. We disconnect from who we want to be, left feeling unworthy, alone, and cut off from our truth.

But here's the thing: **you are not alone**. You're not broken or flawed. We all have an inner saboteur that shames, second-guesses, and tears down our self-worth. And yet, that voice is not the *real you*. We confuse safety with truth. The critic's cruelty feels familiar, so we trust it, even when it hurts.

The Itty Bitty Shitty Committee is just a collection of beliefs we've learned over time. Our negative self-talk echoes how our caretakers, teachers, and even society talked to us in challenging moments. Over the years, those echoes shaped a false self, a version of us that criticizes, judges, compares, and insists we're never enough.

If you meet someone who swears they don't have an Itty Bitty Shitty Committee, either they've done a lot of inner work…or they're an alien. The inner critic sounds different for everyone, but the message is always the same: *you are not enough.*

So let's talk about yours.

One of the easiest ways to spot the Committee is by its grammar and tone. It speaks in the third person, usually starting with "you." *You'll never get it right. You can't do this. You don't belong.*

When it's your true self speaking, you speak in first person. You own the belief: *I did that. I got the job. I ran that marathon.* If we spoke about ourselves in third person, that would just be weird. That's why it's so important to notice the difference. It helps us identify which voice we're listening to and how to disengage from the inner critic.

You know those cartoons with the devil on one shoulder and the angel on the other? The Itty Bitty Shitty Committee is that little devil, whispering in your ear. Its dialogue is negative, merciless, and absolute: *You're not... You could never... You don't... You can't...*

For years, my Committee loved to chime in before every big decision. "You'll embarrass yourself," it would hiss. "Who do you think you are?" Maybe yours sounds different, but it probably knows how to hit exactly where it hurts.

Now pause with me for a moment. Take a deep breath. Place a hand on your heart. Let's get honest about what your Committee says to you when no one's listening:

You're too much... too old... too late... too sensitive...

You're not doing enough...not smart enough...not enough.

You don't have what it takes...you don't have enough time, money, love, courage....

Notice what happens in your body as you read that. Does your chest tighten? Your jaw clench? That's the Committee taking up residence in your nervous system.

Take another breath. Listening to the Itty Bitty Shitty Committee makes us feel truly awful. We would never shame or berate even our worst enemy the way we do ourselves. So breathe into your heart right now. Give yourself grace and remember, this isn't the *real* you. The real you is good. The real you is enough. The real you is the quiet truth beneath all those loud, learned lies.

The 5 C's you'll start learning in Chapter 3 will help you discover your true self, heal unworthiness wounds, and embody your brilliant light. For now, it's enough to simply notice this negative voice and see how it harms your worth. Consciousness is the first agent of change and the doorway to freedom.

The problem with listening to the inner saboteur is that it drags us into a scarcity mindset, a lens that sees only lack and self-centeredness. When fear takes the wheel, love gets shoved into the back seat. When we buy into that scarcity mindset, we believe we'll never be enough or have enough. The cost of listening to this limiting self-talk is that we show up as a smaller version of ourselves, or worse, we don't show up at all. When our inner saboteur runs the show, we lose ourselves, and what's left is shame.

And shame? It thrives in silence.

As Brené Brown teaches, when shame takes over, we start "pleasing, proving, performing, and perfecting" to earn worth instead of remembering we already have it. We do this people-pleasing to compensate for the isolated, unlovable, and unworthy feelings we're left with after the Itty Bitty Shitty Committee has finished chewing us up and spitting us out.

The Itty Bitty Shitty Committee's ringleaders enslaving us in shame are **Comparison, Self-Doubt, Perfectionism,** and **Judgment.** I call them the **Four Horsemen.** Like the Four Horsemen in the Book of Revelation, they bring about our personal apocalypse. They infiltrate our beliefs, chip away at our worth, and sabotage our potential.

The Committee is made up of many voices that destroy our faith in ourselves, but they typically belong to one of these Horsemen. Remember, these voices are not your true self, the real you. They're merely a collection of negative beliefs and judgments you've absorbed from the outside world, reinforced by your conditioned mind.

In this chapter, we'll explore what the Itty Bitty Shitty Committee is, how the Four Horsemen harm your self-worth, and a simple way to help you recognize when you're aligned with the wrong voice. The next chapter will help you discover your true self and how to recognize the real you.

In the rest of this book, I'll guide you through the 5 C's, a set of self-love tools that are your keys to freedom.

But first, let's get to know the Four Horsemen, how they keep us stuck and how to start loosening their grip on your worth.

The Four Horsemen That Sabotage Your Self-Worth

Horseman One: Comparison (I Don't)

We don't have to look very far to feel the tug of our ego comparing us with others. It shows up everywhere: scrolling Instagram and seeing a friend's picture-perfect vacation while you're folding laundry, sitting in a meeting where your coworker lands the promotion you wanted, or watching your best friend glow in her new relationship while you're still swiping through dating apps. Comparison makes our heart ache, pulling us out of our truth and into externals we can't control.

Brené Brown says, "Comparison is the crush of conformity from one side and competition from the other...it's trying to simultaneously fit in and stand out. Comparison says, 'Be like everyone, but better.'"

Comparison whispers: *I don't have enough time... money... resources... skills. I'm not enough.* It does the opposite of what it promises. Instead of connection, it creates separation and disconnection. This is how the Itty Bitty Shitty Committee wins, keeping us stuck in FOMO, scarcity, and smallness.

The more we sit in jealousy or fear, the more it starts to shape how we see everything.

When Comparison takes over, our focus narrows to what someone else has that we don't. We lose sight of what's good and working in our lives, fixating instead on what we lack.

We start rehearsing their highlight reel instead of living our own. Comparison sportscasts our mistakes, shrinking our life into a scoreboard we'll never win. And then, because we're human, we judge ourselves for even feeling jealous in the first place.

It's human to feel envy or longing, but when we dwell there, those thoughts harden into beliefs. The Itty Bitty Shitty Committee's "you" becomes your "I."

Comparison keeps us trapped in *I don't*, and right behind it comes Self-Doubt, whispering *I can't.*

Horseman Two: Self-Doubt (I Can't)

While Comparison measures us against others, Self-Doubt fights a quieter war inside. It questions our abilities, discredits our talents, second-guesses our actions, mistrusts our intuition, and eats away at our self-esteem. Comparison says, "I don't." Self-Doubt says, "I can't."

At first, doubt seems harmless, just hesitation or caution. But left alone, it multiplies. What starts as a whisper becomes a script and soon, we mistake it for truth.

The cost of letting Self-Doubt poison our thoughts is that we don't live up to our true potential. It spins an ongoing story about the person we'll never become, training us into learned helplessness. It calcifies our hearts, burying what is already true and good. When we buy into Self-Doubt, we abandon what is possible for us.

I see this one so often, in my clients and in myself. That moment before you hit "publish," send the email, or ask for help, the voice says, *Don't bother, it won't matter.* And just like that, we abandon ourselves before the world ever could.

Self-Doubt doesn't just question your path, it builds the walls and locks the door.

Horseman Three: Perfectionism (I'm Not Enough)

Perfectionism is critical and cruel. It piles on pressure, forcing us to prove ourselves until we're overwhelmed. Eventually, that pressure becomes paralyzing, and we stop before we even start.

Perfectionism shows up as imposter syndrome and people-pleasing, keeping us trapped in cycles of self-doubt and fear. It makes us construct a pseudo-self, polished on the outside while secretly doubting ourselves on the inside.

That fear of being "found out" keeps us hustling for our worth, pushing ourselves to exhaustion or retreating before we risk being seen. Either way, our creativity suffocates.

When perfectionism runs the show, we don't just fear rejection—we reject ourselves.

Perfectionism also fuels people-pleasing. When we strive to be perfect for everyone, we inevitably try to please everyone, an impossible task. As social creatures, we naturally crave connection and approval. But when our sense of worth depends on keeping others happy, we lose ourselves. Women, in particular, are conditioned to be "good girls," polite, agreeable, self-sacrificing. Over time, this conditioning makes us afraid to disappoint, to take up space, or to assert our needs. The result? We compromise our values, betray our boundaries, and end up resentful. We stay quiet to avoid judgment, dim our light to avoid rejection, and in doing so, chip away at our true selves.

Perfectionism steals the joy from life. It magnifies our flaws, chokes creative momentum, and keeps us stuck in procrastination. Mistakes become failures instead of lessons. Setbacks feel like proof we're not enough. When perfectionism runs the show, we don't just fear rejection—we reject ourselves.

Perfectionism promises belonging but delivers self-abandonment.

Horseman Four: Judgment (I Should/Shouldn't)

At the root of Comparison, Self-Doubt, and Perfectionism is the leader of the Four Horsemen: Judgment.

When neutral, Judgment helps us discern truth from illusion. But when the fearful Itty Bitty Shitty Committee hijacks it, it narrows our perspective, stunts our growth, and walls us off from possibility.

When we judge others, we close ourselves off from ever knowing their potential or receiving their gifts. We assume we already "know" who they are, and in doing so, we miss who they truly are. If you think you already know, you can't grow.

Often, Judgment strikes first to protect us from rejection. It's easier to judge than to risk being seen. But the way we judge others is almost always a mirror of how we judge ourselves.

And nothing cuts deeper than our own self-judgment. It keeps a running scoreboard of how everyone else is doing better. It "shoulds" all over us—who we *should* be, how life *should* look—and traps us in the story of wishing we were someone else, somewhere else.

Rooted in fear of failure or even success, Judgment walls up the heart and chains our courage. It pretends to protect us from pain, but it really locks us away from possibility.

When we release judgment, we release the prison of "shoulds" and finally step toward who we're becoming.

Burn the Book

Maybe your Four Horsemen aren't as blatant or brutal as mine have been. Maybe yours are more cunning and scheming, like *The Plastics*, that clique of bullying high school girls in the movie, *Mean Girls*.

Comparison, Self-Doubt, Perfectionism, and Judgment can be just as vicious. They feed off each other's insecurities, whispering their poison until we start believing them. And just like the Plastics' "Burn Book," shame keeps its own record, pages filled with cruel captions about who we think we are: unworthy, unlovable, too much, not enough.

With their shiny hair and perfect smiles, the Plastics look polished, even enviable. Shame can be that way too, seductive, but toxic. It promises belonging while keeping us in exile from ourselves. It tells us that if we just fix one more thing—our body, our home, our bank account—then we'll finally be enough. But the chase never ends. We get swept up in the noise of doing, proving, scrolling, striving. But deep down, what we really crave is connection. To feel seen. To feel at home within ourselves.

Here's the truth: no one is free from the Itty Bitty Shitty Committee or the shame it fuels. But freedom isn't about silencing it; it's about seeing through its lies. We don't control every thought or emotion, but we can choose which ones we give power to.

The practice of self-love is to become conscious of the voices that aren't truly you, and to choose again...gently, bravely, over and over.

The 5 C's you'll learn in the coming chapters will help you burn your Burn Book, page by page. Set fire to the lies, the "shoulds," and the limiting beliefs that have kept you small. Watch the fire alchemize every story that has kept you captive.

And then, in the stillness among the ashes, be with your whole self—the dark and the light—as you are. Remember that endings aren't failures; they're initiations to a new beginning.

Remember that endings aren't failures; they're initiations to a new beginning.

This is where healing happens, in the quiet recognition that you were never broken, that you were always whole.

Like the blazing phoenix rising from the embers, you can remember who you really are: reborn, worthy, and free.

Signs You've Aligned with the Inner Critic

Now that you've met the Itty Bitty Shitty Committee and its Four Horse-men, let's look at a simple way to spot when it's taken the wheel, and how to take it back. One of my favorite mindfulness metaphors, first popular-ized in conscious-leadership work, is the idea of living "above the line" vs. "below the line."

Imagine an invisible line, what I call **The Alignment Line**. It's the inner threshold between your True Self and your Itty Bitty Shitty Com-mittee; between self-trust and self-abandonment.

The Alignment Line reflects how you're showing up physically, men-tally, emotionally, and energetically. This line isn't about judgment. It's a simple way to become aware of where you are and what's driving you in any given moment.

When you're above the Alignment Line, you're in alignment with your true self, your authentic, ever-expansive, wise, and loving essence. You feel open, free, trusting, grateful, creative, alive. You feel at ease and in rhythm with life. Life feels like it's happening *with* you, not *against* you. That's what it feels like to live above the line, which we'll explore more deeply in the next chapter.

But when you're below the Alignment Line, you're out of alignment with your true self. Below the line is where the Itty Bitty Shitty Committee takes over. You're operating from fear, scarcity, shame, or self-doubt. You're in a state of contraction rather than expansion. You're stuck in self-centeredness versus self-awareness.

Below the line, the Committee loops every mistake, every shortcoming, every way you should be better. Your world shrinks. Your perspective narrows. You see only lack. You armor up, protecting instead of connecting. It's heavy, lonely, and exhausting.

So why do we stay there when it feels so awful? Because our brains are wired to spot danger faster than joy—a gift for survival, but a habit that keeps us stuck in stress.

When we're below the line, our perspective narrows and becomes self-absorbed. Because we're disconnected from our truth, we can't see clearly. Instead of possibilities, we see problems. We might feel inferior or superior, compare, judge, compete, doubt, beat ourselves up, or fear we're missing out. The Committee thrives here, recycling old wounds into familiar spirals.

But here's the key: **consciousness**.

The moment you realize you've dipped below the line, you reclaim your power to choose again, to shift your thoughts, behaviors, and energy and begin returning toward alignment with your true self.

In Chapter 3, we'll deepen this with the first Self-Love Tool, Consciousness, which helps you pause and realign.

For now, let's look at what being below the line *feels* like, so you can start noticing it sooner. There are four main ways your body and spirit send signals: *physical, mental, emotional, and energetic.*

In **The Alignment Line** chart on page 22, you'll find examples of what it can look like when you dip below the line. Use it as a guide, and add your own, so you can begin recognizing how your body and energy speak to you when you're out of alignment with your true self.

- **Physically:** Does your breath get shallow? Shoulders tighten? Stomach churn? Jaw clench?
- **Mentally:** Do you spiral in worry, overthink, or feel foggy and distracted?
- **Emotionally:** Do you flare with anger, sink into shame, or feel resentful, anxious, or disconnected?
- **Energetically:** Do you feel drained, restless, heavy, or overwhelmed?

Ack! Just reading that list probably feels heavy, right? That's the power of energy. These sensations aren't punishments; they're signals showing you that you've slipped out of alignment.

If we don't recognize these signals, we can unconsciously dip further below the line, stuck in emotional loops that feel hard to escape. Thoughts turn into body sensations, which turn into reactions we regret. We keep attracting the same energy we're broadcasting.

But the moment you notice you've dipped below the line, you reclaim your power. Awareness is the doorway back to choice. And with practice, choosing differently becomes easier, bringing you back to your center, your truth, and the loving presence of your true self.

Because the real power isn't in never falling below the line, it's in noticing when you do.

THE ALIGNMENT LINE

Notice when you are above the Alignment Line (aligned with your True Self), or below it (aligned with the Itty Bitty Shitty Committee). Use these as a guide to recognize your own patterns, triggers, and red flags, and add your own.

TRUE SELF

Physical	Mental	Emotional	Energetic
relaxed	clear-minded	at ease	light
free	wise	grateful	in flow
strong	focused	joyful	magnetic
rested	present	compassionate	patient
energized	open	loving	radiant
grounded	creative	balanced	trusting
vibrant	inspired	secure	fulfilled

ITTY BITTY SHITTY COMMITTEE

Physical	Mental	Emotional	Energetic
tight	busy mind	overwhelmed	exhausted
lethargic	foggy	jealous	blocked
clenched	can't focus	fearful	reactive
rapid heartbeat	racing thoughts	anxious	scattered
headaches	ruminating	resentful	depleted
shallow breathing	overthinking	angry	heavy
stressed	doubtful	disconnected	agitated

Return to Center

Consciousness is the first step to change. The moment you notice the red flags signaling you've dipped below the line, you create an opportunity to shift. Rather than letting the Itty Bitty Shitty Committee drive you deeper into self-sabotage, you can pause, breathe, name what you feel, and choose a different response. You have the power to realign with your true self.

Being with your emotions without *becoming* them is an act of conscious self-love. It means witnessing what rises up—anger, fear, shame—without getting dragged into the story. When you notice a trigger, feel it fully in your body and let it move through instead of handing it the keys. Each time you *respond consciously* instead of *reacting unconsciously*, you carve a new path toward inner calm. Over time, those small choices become your way of being.

One simple way to return to your center, especially when emotions run high, is through breathing. *Breathing? Really?* Yes! Intentional breath is a direct path back to presence because it flips your body's "peace switch." The inhale fills you with awareness; the exhale signals your body it's safe to soften. It's the exhale that regulates your nervous system. When we practice slow, rhythmic breathing, we balance the sympathetic and parasympathetic nervous systems, literally shifting the body from stress mode into calm and regulation.

Each time you respond consciously instead of reacting unconsciously, you carve a new path toward inner calm.

Let's try it now. I call this **Coffee Breath** (not to be confused with bad coffee breath). Place one hand on your heart and one hand on your belly. Inhale slowly, feeling your chest and belly rise beneath your palms. Then gently purse your lips into an "O" shape and exhale as if you're blowing on a hot cup of coffee, softly enough not to spill. Continue for 5–10 rounds, letting the exhale be a little longer than the inhale. Intentional inhale.

Effortless exhale. Let each transition be smooth and unhurried as your body and mind relax. Then take a moment to notice how you feel.

I've used this breath everywhere from sitting in traffic to those moments at work when things don't go as planned, and it never fails to reset my nervous system.

Mindfulness is a practice. The more you practice being conscious, the more natural it becomes to notice your patterns in real time without getting caught in the emotional storm. You'll learn even more self-love tools soon, including how to quiet these voices and choose empowering beliefs, but for now, just practice noticing and breathing.

Notice the triggers that pull you off-center and recognize when the inner critic pulls you below the line. Name what you feel, then breathe and sit with it without judgment, without letting it take over. Be with the anger without being angry. Be with the fear without becoming fearful. Become the gentle observer, witnessing your thoughts and emotions without getting swept away in the story's charge. This is the power of witnessing when you're below the line.

Every conscious choice to shift from unconscious reaction to conscious presence is a step toward deeper self-mastery. It takes practice, but over time, these small moments of awareness reshape your patterns and return you to center, so you can live above the line. And each time you return to center, you get a glimpse of the one who's always been there—your true self.

The Gift

The gift of noticing the Itty Bitty Shitty Committee and choosing to stand on your own side is self-awareness. Self-awareness expands you, while self-centeredness contracts you. One opens your perspective; the other keeps you stuck in a narrow, fear-based view of yourself and the world.

Ahimsa, the Sanskrit word for "nonviolence" or "absence of injury," is the first principle in the *Yoga Sutras*, guiding us toward a liberated, conscious life. But ahimsa isn't just about how we treat others. It's also about how we treat ourselves. Every time we believe the Itty Bitty Shitty Committee's harsh narratives, we inflict harm upon ourselves.

If you've been wounding yourself with criticism, doubt, shame, or unkind thoughts, now is the time to choose differently. This shift happens choice by choice, beginning with a simple commitment: to be kinder to yourself in this moment. How can you offer yourself more loving support now? In what ways can you truly have your own back? Practicing ahimsa in your words, thoughts, and actions is the self-love work of liberating yourself.

When you change how you treat yourself, you create a ripple effect that inspires others. When you stand on your own side, you don't just free yourself, you show the world how to love you too. By shifting your perspective, you harness your superpower of conscious choice. By abandoning the Itty Bitty Shitty Committee, you stop abandoning your true self and your potential. Because your story matters. Your voice matters. You matter.

The real gift isn't silencing the critic. It's remembering your true self, the one that knows your worth and calls you to rise above the line.

Integration

The Practice: Notice When You're Below the Alignment Line

Try this: Begin by noticing what it feels like when you're below the **Alignment Line**, when you're aligned with your Itty Bitty Shitty Committee.

Think of a recent moment when you were reactive, triggered, or off-center, when the Itty Bitty Shitty Committee had taken the wheel. Write down what you notice in each of the following areas:

- Physically: How does your body feel when you're below the line?
- Mentally: What kinds of thoughts or stories tend to run through your mind?
- Emotionally: What negative and heavy emotions are most present?
- Energetically: Do you feel contracted, rushed, drained, scattered, or shut down?

This becomes your personal "below the Alignment Line" map.

Now, bring this into your daily life.

Each time you feel triggered, off-center, or reactive, recognize it as a red flag and a clue that you've dipped below the line and aligned with the Itty Bitty Shitty Committee.

When you notice it, take a few slow **Coffee Breaths** and gently return to center.

Reflection:

- What does my Itty Bitty Shitty Committee say to me when I'm below the line?
- What are the most common triggers that pull me below the line?
- If I released a limiting belief or self-sabotaging pattern, what would be available for me?

Muladhara Chakra

Awakening Your Foundation

The Itty Bitty Shitty Committee feeds on fear and disconnection. To rise above it, you first have to feel safe in your body, rooted in your own worth and belonging. That sense of grounded safety begins in your first lower chakra, the root chakra, the energetic foundation for trusting yourself and your life.

In the spiritual physics of yoga, chakras are energy centers that shape our physical, emotional, and spiritual well-being. At the base of the spine lies Shakti, the coiled serpent of divine life force, your untapped potential. When awakened, she rises through the chakras, igniting transformation and guiding you home to your truth.

The root chakra, or *Muladhara* in Sanskrit, is your energetic foundation, your connection to the earth's steadiness and strength. Represented by the color red, it governs your sense of safety, security, and belonging.

When the root chakra is unbalanced, you may feel anxious, ungrounded, or trapped in the Itty Bitty Shitty Committee's fear-based stories. This is when self-doubt takes over and keeps you small. To rebalance, start by pausing and noticing your thoughts. Every time you choose presence over panic, you strengthen your foundation.

Balancing the root chakra means coming home to yourself, trusting that you are safe, supported, and enough. From this rooted place, courage awakens, and your path begins to unfold.

Mantra

I AM SAFE AND SUPPORTED. I AM GROUNDED AND OPEN TO EXPERIENCE ALL THAT I AM.

CHAPTER 2

YOUR TRUE SELF

*"By being yourself, you put something in the world
that was not there before."*

–EDWIN ELLIOT

In 1955 Bangkok, a ten-foot-tall clay statue of the Buddha was being moved to a new temple. On the final attempt to lift it from its pedestal, the ropes snapped, and the statue crashed to the ground. That's when the monks noticed a glimmer of light shining through a crack in the plaster.

Curious, they grabbed chisels and hammers and began carefully chipping away at the thick outer layers. Piece by piece, the glow grew brighter, until finally, they stood in awe at the sight of a solid golden Buddha.

As the story goes, more than two hundred years earlier, monks had covered the statue with plaster and glass to protect it from being looted by an invading army. Their well-kept secret had remained intact until that accident revealed what had been there all along: *pure gold.*

Like those monks who covered their treasure, we also layer ourselves in protection. We add armor around our hearts to shield us from pain and hide our suffering. External layers pile on from other people's judgments, society's expectations, heartbreak, loss, failures, and disappointments. And then there are the heaviest layers of all: the ones we create ourselves. Limiting beliefs. Harsh self-judgments. Fear. Addictions. Attachments. Destructive patterns.

But underneath it all? You are gold. You always were.

But along the way, we forget. We dim our light. We start listening to the inner critic whispering that we're unworthy, broken, or not enough. And we believe the lie. We forget the truth: that we are already radiant, beautiful, unique, and whole.

What are the layers of muck hiding your gold? Is it people-pleasing, perfectionism, over-achieving, self-doubt, or trying to control what's un-controllable? Whatever it is, it's just plaster covering the brilliance that's already you.

What if we saw ourselves the way our Creator sees us? Beautiful. Unique. Irreplaceable. Gold. The 5 C's you'll learn in the coming chapters are your chisels, gently revealing the brilliance that has always lived within you.

The Layers that Cover Your Gold

As children, we're born like the golden Buddha, radiant and bright, with no plaster covering our shine. We come into the world curious, uninhibited, silly, courageous, and full of empathy, honesty, creativity, and love. We trust in goodness. We live in the moment, immersed in wonder at life's surprises and mystery, completely, unapologetically ourselves.

But somewhere along the way, mud gets hurled. Criticism. Disapproval. Disappointment. Harsh words stick to us, seeping into our spirit. We start to question ourselves, doubt our goodness, and bury our gifts. Wanting to fit in, be valued, and belong, we cover our wild, uninhibited nature with conformity. Over time, heartbreak, disappointments, and betrayals add more layers of muck.

The pressure to please and be perfect is the poison. The biggest initiation and invitation is self-trust and permission to be unapologetically you.

The pressure to please and be perfect is the poison. The biggest initiation and invitation is self-trust and permission to be unapologetically you.

When our true self is cloaked in muck, we forget the light we were born with. Instead of living freely, we hustle to become who the Itty Bitty

Shitty Committee says we should be in order to feel worthy and loved. Eventually, we forget the gold is even there. We forget what it feels like to be free, authentic, alive.

And what do we find buried beneath all those layers of shame, regret, anger, anxiety, and grief? Fear. Fear of being judged. Fear of being hurt. Fear of not being enough, of being unlovable, of showing up fully only to be rejected. *Fear...the big ole F-word!*

Fear is sneaky. It lingers in our thoughts, festers in our beliefs, and seeps into our bones. It keeps us closed, numb, and stuck. Fear tells us, "You're too late. You'll fail. Who do you think you are?" And when we believe it, we stay small. Cut off from the magic and joy waiting for us.

The Itty Bitty Shitty Committee loves fear. It feeds on it, keeping us stuck in comparison, sabotage, and judgment, because it knows if we rise into our truth, it loses power.

But here's the thing, our soul work is to gently dissolve those layers of fear and remember who we really are—divine, whole, and already loved. Life is always showing us where we're being invited to grow. And while it's uncomfortable to turn the mirror inward and sit with the emotions we've been avoiding, when we offer ourselves love and safety in those moments, something beautiful happens.

We stop abandoning ourselves. We face our fears, lean into self-trust, and step into new territory. This is how we get unstuck. By embracing the unknown, we grow into who we were always meant to be. By choosing courage over fear, we begin to believe in ourselves again.

Know Thyself

Like the golden Buddha, you have gold waiting to be uncovered beneath the layers. You don't have to look outside for it; the gold is you. Your truth and gifts have always been within. Even if the layers feel thick, everything you seek and need is already inside.

When you quiet the Itty Bitty Shitty Committee's loud chatter, you begin to hear your heart's whisper, uncover your gold, and expand into your innate light.

The Greek philosopher Socrates said, "To know thyself is the beginning of wisdom." In Sanskrit, the term *svadhyaya* means "self-study." What if our work isn't about erasing the Itty Bitty Shitty Committee or trying to be perfect, or even happy? What if it's about practicing svadhyaya to master more of ourselves, not from power over but from a loving power *within*, so we can know ourselves more deeply. To discover the truth of who we *really* are. To remember *all* that we are.

Your true self is always calling you to love your whole self and be free. It is your inner wisdom, your soul, an extension of the Divine, constantly speaking with love, acceptance, and grace. When you feel lost, your true self is the beacon within, guiding you home to your light. Your true self is radiant in her knowing, sovereign in her worth, and rooted in her truth.

You've probably felt this part of you before, those moments when you feel deeply aligned, when life seems orchestrated for you. Because when you're aligned with who you truly are, life begins to move around you and re-arrange in your favor. Opportunities unfold effortlessly. People appear at the right time. Synchronicities happen for you as if the Universe is whispering, "Yes, this way." In this space, life feels like it's happening *for* you, not *to* you. It's knowing that no matter what happens, you are supported, because you are supporting yourself.

So how do we remember our gold when life has us buried under the muck? That's where the 5 C's, the Self-Love Tools come in. When you show up for yourself listening, honoring, and choosing to meet your truth again and again, life reflects that devotion back to you. These tools help you heal conditioned beliefs, listen with trust to your inner wisdom, and live in rhythm with your sacred self. And the deeper your connection to yourself, the deeper your connection to the Divine. The ordinary and the extraordinary alike shimmer with reverence.

Here's the truth: you can't get rid of the Itty Bitty Shitty Committee. That's not the spiritual work anyway. The 5 C's give you a way to partner with yourself instead of battling with your critic. When you choose to love your whole self—the dark and the light, the comfortable and the messy— you begin to see all of it as worthy of gratitude, because all of it is you.

Life will continue to challenge you. You'll rise above and dip below the Alignment Line again and again. But with the 5 C's, you gain perspective. You shift from fear to trust, resistance to acceptance, limitation to possibility.

To know thyself, svadhyaya, is a lifelong practice. A sacred spiral of self-inquiry, reflection, and growth. A beautiful journey of continually shedding what is false to reveal what is true. To see all of you. The path of knowing and loving yourself is the journey and the destination. You will meet yourself again and again—in this moment, the next, and the next— each time touching a deeper truth of who you are.

Take a breath. Feel into what gold you've forgotten. What parts of you are waiting to be seen?

But first, you must clear away the layers that obscure your truth so you can fully remember your gold and shine your light.

The 5 C's: Your Self-Love Tools

The **5 C's** are your soul tools for deeper self-love, your pathway to embodying your fullest, most authentic expression. They help you uncover your light and rise above the line, guiding you back into alignment with your True Self, the part of you that is already sovereign, whole, and worthy. Through these tools, you learn not just to know your worth, but to live it and walk through life rooted in your truth, led by love, with ease and trust.

1. **Consciousness** is the power to step back and see your thoughts and patterns clearly, instead of being run by them. It's how you shift from autopilot to authorship. The gift of consciousness is freedom.

2. **Care** is tending to your inner child, the little one inside you who still carries wounds and limiting beliefs. When you nurture and heal her, you also awaken her natural gifts of play, wonder, and creativity.

3. **Compassion** is how you integrate the rejected and shameful parts of yourself back into wholeness. By being with the shadows instead of running from them, you remember all that you are. The gift of compassion is wholeness and a deeper sense of worthiness.

4. **Curiosity** is letting go of control and leaning into the unknown. It's the bridge from fear to faith, reminding you that you don't need certainty to move forward. The gift of curiosity is trust in yourself and in your path.

5. **Connection** is aligning with your true self and, from that place, feeling deeply connected to others, to your soul's purpose, and the Divine. When you align with who you are meant to be, life flows instead of fights you. Everything becomes sacred. The gift of connection is soul alignment and joy.

Sometimes this soul work feels like actively chiseling through old pain and patterns. Other times, it's a soft surrender, allowing life to unfold, trusting that wisdom rises when you stop forcing. When you release the mental gymnastics, over-efforting, and self-imposed pressure, you clear space for something greater. You rise above the line and back into alignment with who you're meant to be.

Whether you're revealing, shedding, or surrendering, you'll uncover deep emotions and long-held beliefs. There may be moments when you want to retreat. To cover yourself back up, to pretend the gold isn't there. But the work is to stay. Stay with yourself. Sit in the discomfort. Observe without judgment. Trust the process. The only way out is through.

Keep chipping away. Keep aligning. Because what feels heavy now may be the very thing that will set you free.

When you meet yourself with presence, you wake up. You begin to see yourself clearly. And with that clarity comes the deepest remembering: you were never lost. You were never broken.

You've simply been waiting to remember your gold. And now, you will.

Uncovering Your Gold

The story of the golden Buddha is dear to my heart because it reminds us that underneath our thick shells is our own magnificent golden Buddha waiting to be discovered and celebrated. With mindfulness, faith, courage, and love, we have the power to chip away at the layers covering our beautiful, true essence and free our radiant spirit to shine. My friend and writer Courtney J. Burg says, "You have a light within you that's been covered by life. Your only work is to uncover it."

Major life challenges often precede our greatest transformations. My meltdown in Whistler, Canada, that New Year's Eve, revealed many problems in my life, but it also inspired me to set out on a long and winding journey to find meaning. In doing the work of chiseling away heavy layers, I've uncovered gold, my true self, and embraced all my broken parts. I used to try to prove myself. Now, I lovingly try to improve myself. When I catch myself wishing for something different than what I'm experiencing, I do the loving work to meet myself exactly where I am. Is it easy? Heck no! I stumble a lot. But I'm here, present, and moving forward with love.

What about the layers hiding your gold? Your golden Buddha is calling you to get out the chisel and lovingly get to work. Your spirit is calling you to live in alignment with your true self and share the unique gifts that only you have. Imagine what will be available to you when you drop the fears, judgments, and limited beliefs holding you back from unapologetically being YOU.

Each time you chip away at a layer, become aware of your inner saboteur, and consciously choose to transmute your fear into faith, you lay a new path toward the life you desire and the person you want to become, clearing the noise that's been covering your truth.

The mind shouts, but the heart whispers truth. Empty the mind, and open the heart to hear your inner wisdom. And when you slow down enough to listen, you realize the answers were never outside of you. You were never meant to find the path. **You are the path.**

This is the heart of *svadhyaya*: not self-improvement, but sacred remembrance. The gift of aligning with your True Self is seeing *all* of you. Claiming all of you. Trusting the quiet, sovereign wisdom of your true self that has always known the way.

The rest of this book is your sacred remembrance, guiding you home to the gold that has been within you all along.

Integration

The Practice: Notice When You're Above the Alignment Line

Try this: Begin by noticing what it feels like when you're above the **Alignment Line**, when you're aligned with your True Self.

Recall a recent moment when you felt at ease, in flow, grounded, and deeply yourself. Write down what you notice in each of the following areas:

- Physically: How does your body feel when you're above the line?
- Mentally: What is the quality of your thoughts?
- Emotionally: What emotions are present?
- Energetically: Do you feel open, steady, expansive, creative, or alive?

This becomes your personal above The Alignment Line map, a felt sense of your True Self. Begin noticing what helps you slip into this state. When life feels supportive, when you trust yourself, when you feel aligned, pause and let yourself really feel it.

These moments are clues. This is your gold.

Reflection

Close your eyes and take a slow breath. Feel into the energy of your True Self, the version of you who is already whole, free, worthy, and sovereign.

- What does it feel like when I am aligned with my True Self?
- What does my True Self want me to remember?
- What part of my gold is asking to be expressed or honored more fully right now?

Svadhisthana Chakra

Igniting Your Creative Potential

Your True Self is the purest expression of flow and creativity within you. As you connect with her, you awaken the energy of the sacral chakra, the second center of your emotions, desires, and divine creative potential. The sacral chakra, known as *Svadhisthana* in Sanskrit, is located a few inches below the belly button and is associated with the reproductive system, sexuality, emotions, desires, pleasure, and creativity. Represented by the color orange, this chakra governs our ability to flow with life and feel at home in our true self. When this chakra is out of balance, you might feel blocked, rigid, or cut off from your natural flow and creation. Take a moment to notice: are you holding back your desires, creativity, or joy?

To bring this chakra into balance, engage in activities that bring you joy. Create sacred space to listen to your desires, and lean into trusting yourself and your path as a divine being. Remember, you don't need to look outside yourself for answers. They've always been within you.

I AM
CONNECTED
TO MY TRUTH
AND CREATIVE
POTENTIAL.
I HAVE ALL
OF THE ANSWERS
WITHIN ME.
I AM FREE TO
BE ME!

CHAPTER 3

CONSCIOUSNESS

Freeing Yourself from the Inner Critic

"The greatest freedom is to be free of our own mind."
–OSHO

After that first yoga class, I slept uninterrupted for three whole nights. My headaches disappeared, my neck pain softened, and I didn't crave caffeine, sleeping pills, or even excess wine...and Lord knows I love my wine! For the first time in nine years, my mind was clear, and my heart could finally breathe.

But then Monday rolled around, and so did the headaches and that relentless mental chatter. What kind of voodoo was this yoga? Whatever it was, I was hooked. Every Friday at 11:00 a.m., you could find me and a handful of 80-year-old retirees twisting, breathing, and finding our inner Zen.

A few months in, I felt lighter, less cluttered. Before yoga, I'd been spending hundreds of dollars a month on doctors and specialists to fix everything from neck pain to hair loss to psoriasis. Honestly, I was a physical wreck. So when my instructor announced she was leading a 200-hour teacher training, I signed up immediately. It was official: I was on my way to becoming a crunchy, hippie yoga chick, trading in my Manolos for Birkenstocks. (Don't worry, I still shaved my armpits.)

I'd thought yoga was just about movement, but it turned out to be so much more. It was about using our breath, body, and mind to be present. And maybe that was the real problem: I had been living everywhere but the present moment. Every emotion, every uncomfortable truth, had been lodged somewhere deep inside me, buried under my avoidance. By abandoning the present moment, I had been abandoning myself.

My teacher told me the mind is like a wild monkey, what yoga and meditation teachers call "monkey mind." Imagine your head as a house and your mind as a crazy monkey. If left unchecked, the monkey will trash the place. Meditation gives it a job, like focusing on the breath or repeating a mantra, so it can settle down.

I didn't fully get it, but I understood enough. Leave the monkey idle and it will throw its shit everywhere. By 31, that's exactly how my mind felt: chaotic, messy, and full of shit.

Avoiding discomfort and sweeping it under the rug wasn't working. I was tired of being anxious, afraid, disconnected, and lonely. Honestly, I was just tired of being tired.

I craved potency and purpose. I wanted every conversation, every book, every action to matter. To know I mattered. I longed for rest. For play. For more ease within myself. I was seeking more meaning.

And it was seeking me.

Avoiding the present was how I abandoned myself. Consciousness was how I came home.

Lost in the Noise (and the Numbing)

Our world is becoming increasingly fast. Between work, family, and the constant flood of notifications from our devices, life moves at a pace our nervous systems were never built to handle. The steady trickle of dings, emails, and notifications steal our focus, flood our system, and keep us hooked in a relentless cycle of stimulation without satisfaction.

All day long, the mind runs an endless stream of inner dialogue.

The mental math never stops.

It's constantly calculating—what needs to be done, what's coming next, what you forgot, how everything will get handled. One thought triggers another, pulling your attention in a hundred different directions at once.

Out of the tens of thousands of thoughts we think each day, most are recycled, and many lean toward fear, doubt, or self-criticism. The mind's negativity bias once kept our ancestors alive, scanning for danger so they wouldn't be eaten by lions. But today, that same programming keeps us braced, busy, and quietly on edge, even when there is no real threat.

Constantly tracking. Planning. Anticipating.

Our mind is always somewhere else, so we're never fully *here*.

We lose ourselves in two ways: through inner noise and through numbing.

The constant churn of rehashing old stories and worrying about the future keep us distracted, depleted, and disconnected. One unanswered text spins into a story of rejection. A coworker's glance becomes proof they don't like us. Suddenly, we've gone from calm and grounded to an over-reactive cave dweller armed with a smartphone and a stress response.

Did you know an emotional charge in the body only lasts about 90 seconds? After that, it's not the *feeling* that hurts; it's the *story* we keep replaying long after the moment has passed.

And when we're not caught in that story, we reach for distraction instead.

Have you ever picked up your phone to research something, and ten minutes later found yourself down a rabbit hole or mindlessly scrolling social media? We scroll, snack, overwork, or busy ourselves in an attempt to escape discomfort or to feel something, anything, different. As the author Jonathan Haidt says, "the devices are our relationship blockers and presence blockers." These distractions become unconscious addictions that disconnect us from the present moment, from each other, and from ourselves.

Whether we're stuck in the internal noise of the Itty Bitty Shitty Committee or caught in the numbness of distraction, we're missing our life, because we're missing the present moment. And the ache beneath all of this, the question we're really asking, is simple and human: *Do I matter?*

It's only in the present moment that we can feel the answer. Only *here in the now* can we feel joy, meaning, connection, aliveness, and purpose—not as ideas, but as lived experience.

It begins with consciousness.

Self-Love Tool #1: Consciousness

Consciousness is the first tool we use to get unstuck from the mind's chatter and return to the present moment. Our power lies only here, now.

Consciousness helps you notice when you've dipped below the Alignment Line and are misaligned with your true self. It's a practice of being mindful and present instead of reactive, scattered, and stressed. It's how you interrupt the spin, pause instead of reacting, and choose again from a more aligned place.

Consciousness isn't a destination. It's a devotional practice. Each moment is an invitation to return to the present.

Consciousness isn't a destination; it's a devotional practice.

Even if the experience you're in isn't what you want, presence is the pathway to healing the emotions around it. You don't have to *like* the moment to be with it, you just have to stay. Being present helps you remain in your power. Responding instead of reacting. Grounded instead of scattered.

And as the great late spiritual teacher Wayne Dyer said, "A miracle is simply a shift in perspective."

Consciousness brings you into the present moment, where your perspective can shift, where your lens widens and you're able to see something new that wasn't available before. This act of awareness is where the miracle happens.

Consciousness is your superpower because it gives you choice. Each time you choose to be present—to pause, notice, and respond from awareness rather than habit—you rise above the Alignment Line and move back into alignment with your true self, instead of defaulting to the Itty Bitty Shitty Committee's well-worn path. That's how new neural pathways and a new way of being are formed.

Sometimes our transformation unfolds slowly, layer by layer. And sometimes it happens in an instant, when we see the moment differently. That shift in perspective is the miracle of being conscious.

With practice, returning to the moment becomes a way of being. Over time, those small moments of awareness shape how you live.

Consciousness: The Practice of Staying

Consciousness is the practice of staying present, even when it's uncomfortable, when every instinct tells us to run, numb, or distract ourselves. Most of us were never taught how to sit with discomfort. We were taught to push through, fix, or avoid it. But true awareness means staying with yourself in those moments, noticing what's happening without judgment, and letting it be exactly as it is.

I was at the grocery store one morning when I heard screeching and yowling. The sound was so intense that I had to look around for the source. It turned out to be a little boy, maybe two years old. His face was red with hysteria. I could only imagine what set him off. Was he denied the OREO® cookies he wanted? *I get it, kid. Those cookies are pure heaven. Seriously, who can believe they're vegan?*

His loud bawling went on for what felt like twenty minutes. While everyone in the store looked away, his mom kept hastily loading her cart. When I ended up behind them at checkout, I felt for this child. Yes, he was being a pest, and we were all semi-annoyed, but underneath his protest, he was having big, uncomfortable emotions and just wanted to be seen and heard.

Staying present with our unwelcome emotions is like being the parent of a toddler mid-tantrum. If you ignore the child, he'll cry louder and make a bigger scene. If you try to rush a solution, it won't work because the emotions are too wild to be tamed quickly. The best thing you can do is stay present, breathe, and empathize. No need for words. Just be there.

It's hard, of course. You want that child to quiet down, and fast. But when you stay with him—listening, accepting, not judging, and not needing to fix anything—the emotions will peak and eventually soften. And when they do, connection happens. He feels safe again, because you stayed.

The same goes for our emotions. Most of us parent them the way we were parented: with distraction, denial, or control.

Like that toddler, your difficult emotions simply want to be seen, heard, and accepted. Each time you choose awareness and lovingly stay with your emotions, you rise above the line and get to know your whole self. You free the emotions to create space for a meaningful response, and that space is where healing happens.

This is where consciousness steps in, turning awareness into choice, and choice into freedom.

While we can't control what emotions get triggered, we can control how we meet our thoughts and emotions in the present moment. Consciousness gives us that meeting place. It helps us notice our patterns, interrupt the spin of the Itty Bitty Shitty Committee, and return to presence, where clarity and ease live.

So how do we stay with what is when everything in us wants to run? We practice.

Three Ways to Practice Consciousness

Meditation, Sacred Stillness, and what I call the Power of the Pause are three ways to practice consciousness. **Meditation** creates space in the mind, helping us be more present and less reactive. **Sacred Stillness** helps us feel more grounded so we can see the awe and beauty around us. And the **Power of the Pause** helps us calm down when we're triggered, so we can respond consciously and intentionally instead of react unconsciously.

These are not one-time tools; they're daily devotionals that help us return home to ourselves, over and over again.

Let's begin.

Meditation

When I first started meditating, my mind was like a war zone. Time crawled. I'd sit there breathing while my thoughts threw a rager in my head. But over time, as I practiced sitting with my unruly thoughts and burning emotions, without reacting or judging, I started to see a pattern. Those endless loops of fear and judgment weren't the real me. They were just noise. The more I sat with myself, the more I began to meet myself.

Meditation isn't about stopping your thoughts, forcing positivity, or turning into a blissed-out monk. It's simply about watching your thoughts without getting swept into their drama. It's like sitting on a riverbank, watching the water flow by, instead of jumping in and being carried downstream.

When you stop getting carried away by your thoughts, you create a little space between yourself and them. This gap is where consciousness lives. It's where you realize: you are not your thoughts. You're the one witnessing them.

Thoughts will always come and go. Meditation gives you a pause between stimulus and response. That gap gives us space between reacting from a triggered emotion and responding from presence. It helps us move away from our self-centered, limited thinking and expand our perspective into more self-reflection and self-awareness.

I'll be honest, meditation sucks at first. It's like working out: painful...until it's not. At first, your mind will do anything to avoid stillness. It will suddenly remember laundry or emails, or pull you into your to-do list. That's okay. The practice isn't about stopping your thoughts; it's about noticing that you're not them.

And no, this doesn't turn you into an emotionless robot. Quite the opposite. When you meet the moment *as it is*, you actually feel more alive, because you're no longer tangled in the Itty Bitty Shitty Committee's stories.

Meditation is something we practice in solitude so we can live it out in the real world. It frees us from the Committee's toxic grip and helps us expand into our true self, connected to everything around us in a deeper way. Each time you practice sitting with your thoughts without fixing, running, or indulging them, you strengthen the muscle of awareness. So when life gets loud, you can return to your center faster.

As the mental noise softens, something else becomes easier to feel...your heart and your truth. You don't force this openness; it happens naturally when you stop chasing every thought or forcing every answer. In that quiet space, presence becomes possible. And presence is what opens the heart.

In the book, *The Untethered Soul*, Michael Singer compares the mind's chatter to a roommate who never shuts up. Imagine this roommate following you around, saying out loud everything you silently say to yourself.

She wakes you up by announcing your to-do list. She critiques your body in the mirror: *Wow, you really let yourself go. You shouldn't have had that wine last night. Is that a new wrinkle?* She nags you on your commute, trails you through work, replays every conversation, spirals into worst-case scenarios, and critiques your every move. At night, she crawls into bed with you, whispering until you finally pass out.

If this were an actual person, you'd call the cops. But you can't, because the roommate is you!

As Singer puts it: "There is nothing more important to true growth than realizing that you are not the voice of the mind…you are the one who hears it."

And that's the gift of meditation: it's how you break up with the psycho roommate and reclaim the peace and power of your true self.

If you'd like to explore guided practices, I've created free meditations for you at www.audreysuttonmills.com, each one designed to help you quiet the Committee, open your heart, and remember the sacred soul you really are.

Sacred Stillness

The second way to quiet the mind's chatter and hear the heart's whispers is to find moments of sacred stillness throughout your day. These are the pauses that pull you out of your to-do list and mental math and back into your life. It's as simple as hearing the birds chirp, noticing the warmth of sunlight on your skin, or feeling your feet on the ground while waiting for your coffee to brew.

Without these intentional moments, life's demands pull us. But when we carve out sacred stillness, we allow ourselves to rest, reset, and renew. These small pauses create space for your soul to breathe. They offer a break from the noise and a doorway back to your intuition.

Imagine your mind as a lake. Thoughts ripple across the surface, and when the mind is cluttered, the water turns choppy and murky. But with sacred stillness, the waters settle. The lake grows clear and still, reflecting the sun, the moon, and the stars, a mirror for the beauty of life itself.

When I find myself rushing, I pause and breathe until the water clears again.

Sacred stillness quiets the mind and opens the heart. It widens our lens and invites us back into life's wonder. By pausing, we pick up our heads from the grind and finally see the awe that was here all along: the way sunlight dances on leaves, the laughter of a child, the simple miracle of being alive.

Awe is sacred stillness in motion. It reminds us that we are part of a miraculous world, one planet spinning in a galaxy that belongs to an infinite universe. When we slow down, awe finds us.

Children have an innate sense of wonder. As adults, the busyness of life dulls that sense, and we forget to pause long enough to let awe in. Making time for awe is a practice that helps us slow down and open our eyes to the magic around us and within us. Studies show that awe helps us feel more calm, connected, and joyful.

Paulo Coelho wrote, "The simple things are also the most extraordinary things. Only the wise can see them." Awe is everywhere and can easily be experienced by becoming present to the world around you: a golden sunset that stops you in your tracks, the smell of rain, the taste of fresh air, the sound of your own laughter.

Awe pulls us out of the inner critic's narrow, self-centered view and returns us to reverence for life's magnificence.

And if you ever feel stuck, step outside. Nature is awe's greatest teacher, inviting you out of the narrow perspective of the mind and back into the expansive harmony of life.

Taking time for sacred stillness is a profound act of self-love. It's like sitting down with an old friend, the kind who lets you take off the mask and just be. In this stillness, you feel your light return. You reconnect with yourself, with life, and with the quiet, steady voice within that knows exactly what you need.

The more you honor these moments of sacred stillness, the more mindful and present you become. Soon, life feels less hurried and far more harmonious. A dance between *doing* and *being,* where your intuition speaks, your heart listens, and your truth gently leads the way.

The Power of the Pause: Notice, Pause, Choose

Because modern life will always push you to speed up and keep up, the third way to practice consciousness is through the **Power of the Pause**. Life isn't always rainbows and unicorns. Your thoughts, energy, and actions will naturally ebb and flow above and below the Alignment Line. Something will trigger you, and the Itty Bitty Shitty Committee will try to send you into a tailspin. The pause helps you interrupt the spiral and return to your true self.

The Power of the Pause comes down to three simple steps: **Notice. Pause. Choose**.

Notice

Awareness is the first step. Begin by simply noticing when your energy shifts: when your breath shortens, your chest tightens, or your thoughts start to spiral below the line. These are your red flags, your body's way of whispering, *Hey love, something's off.*

When you catch yourself in that swirl, pause for just a moment before reacting. Instead of getting swept into the story, name what's here: I'm angry. I'm hurt. I'm anxious. That simple act of naming brings you back to now. It validates what you feel and loosens the critic's grip.

You can use your **Alignment Line** from Chapter 1 here to check in with how your triggers show up in your body, emotions, mind, and energy. These cues are your internal compass, letting you know when you've dipped below the line.

Your red flags might look like:

- Body: tight jaw or shoulders, shallow breathing, heat in the chest.
- Mind: worst-case forecasting, absolute words like always or never.
- Energy: urgency, frantic fixing, or that pull to people-please.

Each time you notice, you've already shifted. You've stepped into consciousness. The next step is to pause.

Pause

In the pause, you create sacred space for choice. Even five deep breaths can disrupt an old, reactive pattern. Try taking five slow *Coffee Breaths*: five deep inhales, five long exhales, and feel your nervous system catch up with your heart. That's how you reset, in real time. Pausing softens heated emotions and lets you sit with your feelings without letting them take the wheel. In this gap between trigger and reaction, you can validate your emotions while keeping them in the passenger seat. The pause brings you back to presence, the only place peace lives.

Choose

Once you've noticed and paused, you're ready to choose a thought or action that serves you. That might look like stepping outside, journaling, calling a friend, or dancing it out. Every conscious choice moves you closer to peace and helps you rise above the line.

Peace begins with you: your thoughts, actions, and beliefs, in this moment. When you shift your perspective, you transform your experience.

The more you practice pausing, the more you'll recognize the difference between the voice of your Itty Bitty Shitty Committee and the truth of your higher self. Start with the small triggers—the traffic, the text, the tone—and build your pause muscle for the bigger storms.

Peace begins with you: your thoughts, actions, and beliefs, in this moment. When you shift your perspective, you transform your experience.

The power of the pause gives you space in your mind and breath in your body. What you do with that choice becomes your embodied practice.

When You're Triggered: Five Quick Choices

When fear, judgment, or scarcity pull you below the line, you don't need to "fix" everything. You just need one conscious choice. When you practice consciousness through meditation, stillness, and the power of the pause, you create space from the mind to return to your heart.

The practices below are simple ways to realign when you notice you're off-center. You don't need to master all of them. Choose one and practice it this week.

1. Change The Channel

Attuning to your heart, rather than your mind's fear-based chatter, is a quick way to rise above the line and align with your true self. The Itty Bitty Shitty Committee is loud, bossy, and relentless, echoing all the critical voices you've absorbed over the years. But beneath that noise is a gentler voice, the voice of your true self: your heart.

Your heart doesn't scream, it whispers. It offers compassion, creativity, and the deep knowing that you'll be okay. When you listen closely, you feel clarity, openness, and peace. That's your soul's loving guidance, your deeper truth.

When you catch yourself slipping below the line, try "changing the channel." It's like turning the dial from a static-filled station to one playing your favorite song, the one your soul already knows by heart. Pause and notice what your inner critic is saying. Write down what the Committee says. Then place your hand on your chest, take a few deep breaths, and ask: *What does my heart know to be true?*

This simple practice shifts you out of the Itty Bitty Shitty Committee's grip and back into alignment with your heart's wisdom. The mind's chatter keeps us stuck in fear and judgment, but the heart's whisper sets us free. It shows a clearer path forward, always with love. Each time you attune to your heart, you return to the part of you that is eternally loving, supportive, and wise.

2. Question the Inner Critic (and Reclaim Your Power)

The inner critic loves to nag: *You are not enough. You can't do this. You don't deserve that.* When those voices show up, don't just buy in. Get curious.

Ask yourself:

- Is this really true? Or is this just an old, conditioned belief on repeat?

If it does feel true, ask: *Is it true all the time?* This softens the critic's harsh absolutes and makes the voice less intimidating.

Here's a twist: when the negative self-talk tape starts to play, interrupt it with what I call a **negative mantra**. I know, it sounds backwards, but stick with me. Instead of forcing a positive affirmation you don't believe (I'm confident!), use a statement that feels powerful and true.

Research by Dr. Vanessa Patrick from the University of Houston found that reframing "I can't" as "I don't" increases our sense of agency, nearly three times more effective than saying "no," and eight times more powerful than "I can't." Saying "I don't" feels like a choice rather than a restriction.

So when your mind starts spinning with future to-dos, try: "I don't do overwhelm." When you're about to speak up and that old voice whispers "Who do you think you are?" meet it with: "I don't do self-doubt." And when you catch yourself replaying a conversation for the fifth time, dissecting every word, try: "I don't do overthinking."

Let me give you a real-life example. I have a thing for donuts (and chips, but donuts, man, they get me!). Sometimes, when I'm halfway through a donut, I'll catch myself and say, "I don't do self-sabotage." And there have been times, true story, when I've literally put the donut down and walked away. Not always (I'm human too!), but more often than not, this mantra interrupts my pattern and helps me make a better choice to rise above the line.

Why does it work? Because even though it uses "negative" phrasing, it disrupts old conditioning and asserts a new truth. It's like holding up a hand to your inner critic and saying, *Nope, thanks for your input, but I'm driving now.*

Try it: What's one story you're done believing? Flip it into an "I don't" mantra and say it out loud. Notice how it shifts your energy.

When you question the inner critic or choose a new mantra, you reclaim your agency and your peace.

3. Practice Active Acceptance

Active acceptance is the practice of embracing the moment as *it is*. It stops the spiral of blame and judgment and realigns you with your true self.

Our attachment to control—how we think life *should be* and how others *should* behave—creates our suffering and keeps us stuck below the line. When we resist the flow of life by trying to control it, we unhinge from our true self.

Active acceptance is not passive or weak; it's choosing to meet the present moment as it is, without giving up on your goals or allowing others to mistreat you. What you're releasing is the critic's story, bias, blame, and shame. Active acceptance is courage and presence.

It's releasing blame and comparison, taking responsibility for your life, and recognizing that every experience has a divine purpose, even when it's unclear. This shift from looking outside yourself to softening within restores your sense of agency, empowerment, and peace.

We're human, and our ego likes to feel in control. Whether it's managing your partner, replaying old conversations, mapping out the future, or holding yourself to unspoken expectations, this is how the Committee drags you back into the story. Active acceptance invites something different. It asks you to meet the moment *as it is*. When you do, you take ownership of your life. *I didn't get the job. He didn't text back. I'm upset. Okay. Now what?*

That surrender isn't giving up. It's releasing the grip of *should* so you can rise with clarity and choose your next step. Judgment shrinks us. Acceptance frees us.

Try this: set a "no-judgment hour." For sixty minutes, notice every judgment of yourself, others, or a situation. Label it "judging," breathe, and return to neutral. Instead of getting swept into the story, practice pausing from judgment and choosing peace. The more you practice, the more you free yourself from the Committee's cyclone of *shoulds* and rise with ease.

4. Practice Appreciation

Appreciation is a portal to joy. True appreciation immediately bridges the gap between below the line and above the line feelings because gratitude and resentment can't coexist. This isn't about faking gratitude or slapping on a smile. It's about choosing how you want to feel, even in the middle of the mess.

Usually, we're grateful *after* we receive what we desire. The problem is, that keeps us powerless, forever chasing the next thing we think will finally make us happy. What if, instead of waiting for joy, we practiced joy *now*?

By consciously practicing appreciation in the moment, we become the energy we desire, and that energy attracts more of the same.

You can practice appreciation by focusing on what's working in your life right now: the breath in your lungs, the people who love you, or the challenges you've walked through that revealed your strength. Even your hardest seasons become proof of how resilient you are, far more than the Committee would have you believe.

And when you've dipped into scarcity or comparison, look for the "driftwood." As spiritual teacher, Abraham Hicks calls it, "driftwood" are the signs, synchronicities, and even other people's successes that drift into your awareness. Instead of comparing and sinking further below the line, see that driftwood as evidence that what you desire is possible for you too. That you're already on the right path because you can see it.

Appreciation is how we stop spiraling below the line and choose abundance instead. It's simple, but it works every time.

5. Follow What Feeds Your Spirit

When you're out of alignment with your true self, it's often because you've neglected the flame within, the spark of creativity and joy that keeps you alive and vibrant. The quickest way back above the Alignment Line is to do something that makes you feel alive and light, no matter how small.

Your spirit is the part of you that knows joy is your birthright. Maybe it's the song that makes you dance in the kitchen, the belly laugh you share with a friend, the spark of creativity when you let yourself play, or the quiet exhale when you finally rest. These are whispers of your spirit, calling you back into alignment.

Even a few moments of choosing what nourishes instead of numbs can shift everything from your mood, your energy, your perspective. Each time you follow joy instead of judgment or pressure, you rise.

When you listen to your spirit and let it lead, it will always guide you back into alignment with your true self, into joy, freedom, and worthiness.

Okay, let's pause for moment and take a breath. I just shared a lot of ways to realign with your true self when you slip below the line. Remember, consciousness is a practice, not a destination. Each time you choose awareness over autopilot, old patterns begin to dissolve.

A new way of thinking and being becomes your natural state bringing more ease, harmony, and alignment. Take what works and leave the rest. Start with one of these practices when your emotions get activated. Once it feels natural, add another.

Consciousness isn't a quick fix; it's a way of living. And every time you rise above the line, you come home to who you've always been.

What this looks like in real life

We've all had this kind of day: a terrible night's sleep, you oversleep, skip breakfast, and rush out the door. On the drive to work, you white-knuckle the steering wheel, weaving through crawling traffic, desperate to find the fastest lane. When a car cuts you off, coffee spills all over your shirt, making you even more late for your meeting. Your stress rises, and without even realizing it, you carry that mood into work, can't focus, and by the time you crawl into bed that night, you're just hoping tomorrow will somehow be better.

Imagine another version of the same day. This time, you get a good night's sleep because you read a book the night before instead of scrolling on your phone. You wake up naturally, feeling refreshed and grounded. Instead of grabbing your phone first thing, you close your eyes, take a few deep coffee breaths, and spend ten minutes in meditation.

These small practices give your mind space. Then, in a moment of sacred stillness, sipping your tea slowly, hand on heart, you set an intention for the day.

On the drive to work, a car cuts you off. Your heart rate spikes and your shoulders tense, but this time, you notice the red flags. So, you pause, take a few long exhales, and repeat your negative mantra: *I don't do overwhelm.* This interrupts the rush of reactivity. You turn on your favorite podcast, laugh out loud, and feel the tension ease from your body.

Later, your partner calls to say he has to work late and asks you to pick up the kids. The Committee fires up fast: *Of course. It's always on me!* You feel irritation tighten in your chest. But instead of stewing and listening to the inner critic's blame loop, you take a breath and **change the channel**, tuning into the whisper of your heart. The soft voice of compassion says,

Let go of resentment and meet the moment now. Everyone is doing their best. So you order pizza and go with the flow.

You move through the day differently. Instead of carrying stress into every room, you create moments that feed your spirit: stepping outside for a breath of fresh air and noticing the sunset before you walk back inside. By evening, you're more present with your family, more at ease in your own body, and more connected to yourself. You end your day reflecting on three things you're grateful for.

In this version, you practiced consciousness in real life. Not perfectly, but intentionally. This is how we stop living on autopilot and begin rising above the line, guided by clarity, presence, and choice. The more you practice, the more your inner world shifts. It's not about perfection; it's about practice. And with practice, presence becomes easier. Harmony and joy become more familiar. Alignment with your true self becomes something you return to more easily, again and again.

The Gift

The gift of consciousness is freedom from the Itty Bitty Shitty Committee and the old conditioning that once ran your life. Through practices like meditation, sacred stillness, and the power of the pause, you quiet the noise, soften the false stories, and reconnect with the truth of who you are.

Consciousness gives you choice. Fear softens into faith. Constriction gives way to trust. You transform self-centeredness and scarcity into deeper self-awareness and abundance. You start to hear your intuition clearly and feel supported by the greater Source guiding you.

With these practices, you begin to see differently: obstacles become invitations, triggers become teachers, losses become lessons, and problems reveal new possibilities. The depth of presence you bring to each moment opens your awareness in ways that change everything.

Consciousness isn't a single awakening; it's a continual homecoming. Each time you notice, breathe, and return to the moment, you meet life with softer eyes and a steadier heart. The more you practice, the more natural it becomes. Through consciousness, you begin to create a life of clarity, ease, and meaning, one that feels aligned with your true self.

Now, as you create space from reaction and rest in awareness, you may begin to feel the old wounds and tender places that never received the care they needed. This is the next step of your journey, learning to meet those parts with tenderness. That's where Care comes in, the second self-love tool. Consciousness is awareness. Care is love in action.

Because true freedom isn't just quieting the noise. It's learning to nurture the wounded places within so you can remember the light that's always been yours.

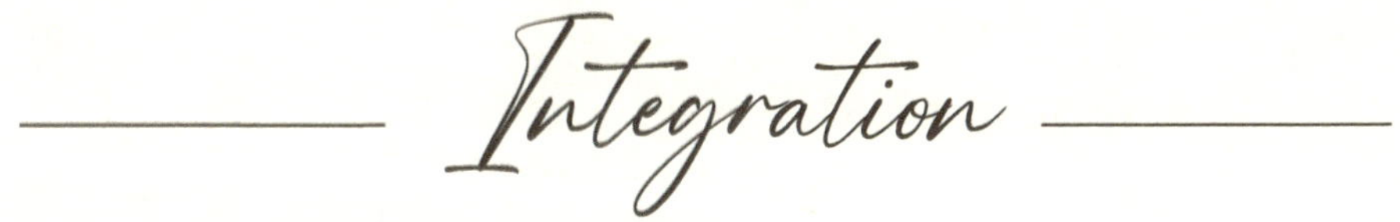

Integration

The Practice

Try this practice anytime you notice yourself slipping below the Alignment Line.

Notice when you're triggered or getting lost in story, when your breath shortens, your body tenses, or your thoughts start to spiral. Name it as a red flag: *I'm below The Alignment Line.*

Pause and place one hand on your heart. Feel your feet on the ground. Take a few slow breaths, letting the exhale soften your body and bring you back to now.

Choose to turn toward your heart, the part of you that is wise, grounded, and loving, instead of following the Itty Bitty Shitty Committee's commentary. Ask yourself, *What does my heart need now?* Listen, and choose one small way to support yourself in rising above the Alignment Line.

Each time you notice, pause, and choose, you strengthen the muscle of consciousness. You rise above the line and align with the truth of who you are, calm, clear, and connected. Presence becomes power, one conscious breath and one loving choice at a time.

Reflection

- Where am I resisting what *is*?
- What becomes possible when I pause instead of react?
- What does my heart know when I'm fully present?

Manipura Chakra

Igniting Our Inner Fire

The *Manipura*, or solar plexus chakra, sits a few inches above your belly button. Represented by the color yellow, it governs your inner fire (agni), your will, and your confidence. When this chakra is out of balance, your inner fire dims, you may feel uncertain or lose your spark.

This is your power center, your personal sun. When it's bright, you feel confident, purposeful, and aligned with your truest self.

Shakti, your creative life-force energy, can get stuck in the lower chakras, keeping you looping in old thoughts or behaviors. Consciousness is what liberates this energy, helping you move beyond old patterns and return to freedom.

To balance this chakra, bring awareness to your thoughts and patterns. Notice where your energy contracts or where you dim your light. Consciousness helps you digest experiences and emotions and choose a new way forward.

Each time you return to presence, your energy flows freely again. Conscious choice is your superpower reigniting your inner flame. When you rise above the line and return to alignment, you reconnect with who you innately are: your truest, freest, fullest self.

WHEN I'M IN CONSCIOUSNESS, I'M IN CHOICE. I AM THE POWERFUL AUTHOR OF MY OWN STORY.

CHAPTER 4

CARE

Becoming a Safe Place Within

"The nature of unconsciousness is such that, until it's metabolized, it will seep through generation after generation. Only through awareness can the cycle of pain that swirls in families end."

—DR. SHEFALI TSABARY

I remember one particular drive home from school with my dad when I was seven years old, the day I tried to assert my independence. The details of our argument are blurry, but the way he handled it, and the betrayal I felt, are still crystal clear.

My dad was the kindest person with the biggest heart, but he was also human and had a temper. Whatever I had said must have offended him. In our house, *tone* was a big deal. He pulled the car to the side of the road, turned toward me, and locked eyes with me.

"Apologize. Right now."

My stomach churned. I didn't want to apologize. I felt I was right. I was a big girl, and I believed it was time to stand up for myself. I swallowed hard and timidly stammered, "No."

His expression hardened. "What did you just say to me?"

"No. I . . . I don't think I need to apologize." My voice wavered; more of a question mark than a mic drop.

His jaw tightened. "Say you're sorry. Right now."

Something in me knew this moment mattered. My dad was a kind and generous person, sometimes to a fault. But the worst thing you could do to him? Disrespect him. And right now, he saw my refusal as exactly that.

"Audrey," he repeated, his voice low and firm, "say you're sorry."

I took a deep breath and held my ground. "No, Dad. I don't think I should say I'm sorry if I'm not sorry."

The air in the car changed. His face darkened and his frustration showed. "Then you're grounded." Without another word, he hit the gas and sped back onto the road.

Tears stung my eyes, but I clenched my jaw, willing myself not to cry. My dad and I had always been best friends. He was the person I laughed with, the one I shared my wildest ideas with. Every day, I felt his love for me. He lived for our family. My dad told me constantly that I was his biggest joy. But in this moment, that love suddenly felt uncertain to my seven-year-old heart.

And that is when a new belief began to take root inside me, a quiet message absorbed in that moment: *maybe it wasn't safe to speak up after all.*

Decades later, I told my dad this story. Tears welled in his eyes as his face fell. He did not remember it. His voice was thick with remorse when he finally said, "That makes me sound like a bad father."

He was not. He was my world, and I was his. Our relationship was filled with laughter, warmth, and deep connection. This moment was not the story of my childhood. It was one small moment that left an imprint on a sensitive seven-year-old nervous system, as small moments sometimes do.

But as an adult, I can see him with more clarity and empathy. My dad carried his own childhood wounds of being unseen by an emotionally neglectful father. Like many of us, he was navigating patterns passed down through generations. Like many passionate people, when emotions ran high his temper could flare, but he always apologized. He deeply desired to be self-aware, and his heart was in the right place.

The truth is, as humans we begin forming our responses to conflict and emotion very early in life. When we experience tension, rejection, or disconnection, our nervous system instinctively moves into survival responses of fight, flight, or freeze. These reactions are how we learn to navigate the world.

The thing is, as children we don't yet have the capacity to understand our parents' pain or see them as complex human beings. We simply *feel* the impact of what happens around us.

If our behavior is "rejected," we often *feel* rejected too. And when our emotions are corrected or shut down instead of being understood, we can internalize that experience deeply. As children, we don't separate the behavior from the self. We don't think, *My behavior was wrong.* We often *feel, Something about me must be wrong.*

Self-doubt creeps in, then self-blame, then shame.

Those early interpretations don't simply disappear with age. They quietly travel with us into adulthood, showing up as self-doubt, people-pleasing, perfectionism, or a fear of speaking our truth.

Looking back, that drive home planted a quiet belief in me. Somewhere inside, I began to wonder if my opinions and feelings were safe to express.

Like many families, we did not always know how to hold big emotions. So I became a master chameleon, adapting to what others needed instead of learning what I needed from myself.

This memory hit me differently when I told my dad the story because I was twenty weeks pregnant with my first child, wondering what kind of mother I would become. Life was no longer just about me. Even though I had a childhood filled with love, I was afraid of becoming a parent who didn't know how to lovingly hold space for difficult emotions.

But here is the truth: it wasn't my parents' fault. They were human, doing the best they could with the awareness they had. They parented me with love and the intention to raise a strong, capable daughter.

Whether our childhood was loving or painful, we all inherit ways of responding to the world from what was modeled.

How they talked to us and treated us as children is often how we talk to and treat ourselves as adults. Unless we become aware of our patterns, it's easy to repeat what hasn't yet been repaired. We parent the way we were parented.

> *Unless we become conscious of our patterns, we repeat what's not repaired.*

But consciousness gives you choice. And choice is your superpower. You get to be the cycle breaker.

Before we go deeper, I want to say something gently. Inner child work can bring up big emotions. Sometimes it stirs sadness, anger, or even shame about the past. If that happens, be tender with your heart.

This work is not about blaming our parents or condemning our childhood. It's also not about judging ourselves if we are parents. It's an invitation to meet our stories with honesty, curiosity, and compassion. It invites us into deeper awareness and reflection for ourselves and those who raised us so we can release what no longer belongs to us and feel free to be fully ourselves.

Many of us were raised in loving homes by caregivers who truly did the best they could with the awareness they had. Healing is not about pointing fingers. It's about caring for the younger part of ourselves who did not yet have the understanding we have now.

In this chapter, we'll explore the soul tool of **Care** and how to nurture your inner child and heal the beliefs you learned when you were young. The voices of the Itty Bitty Shitty Committee are often echoes of the past, reflections of what we were taught about our worth. But when you learn to care for your inner child, you can heal the shame, the pain, and the unspoken rules that told you your feelings were too much.

Through reparenting, you will learn to nurture and support your inner child, so that the loving adult within you can finally care for the younger parts of your heart that still long for understanding.

Generational Wounds: Where Our Beliefs and Behaviors Began

Before we explore how to care for the inner child, let's gently look at where these wounds came from and why they still live in us today. The truth is, many of our fears, insecurities, and patterns didn't start with us. They were passed down like emotional heirlooms.

This isn't about blame. It's about awareness. When we recognize what was modeled to us, we get to decide what we want to keep and what we're ready to release.

And what we inherit doesn't have to be overtly traumatic to leave a mark. Many of us absorbed invisible patterns such as codependency, perfectionism, people-pleasing, emotional suppression, and overachieving long before we had words for them.

As children, we learn what love is from our caregivers through how it was expressed in our homes and environments. We watched how our parents handled stress, conflict, affection, disappointment, and repair. What we witnessed became our earliest relational blueprint.

You may have grown up in a home where everything looked fine, stable, loving, even privileged. Yet underneath, you learned quiet lessons like:

Feeling deeply is dangerous.

Crying is weak.

Love must be earned.

Conflict is something to fear.

You can be accepted, but only if you hide the messy parts.

As children, especially before age seven, we don't have the capacity to process emotions or make sense of the world. We absorb the energy, reactions, and patterns of the adults around us. Their voice becomes our inner dialogue. Their fears become our nervous system. Their beliefs become our blueprint.

We learn, often without words, what brings connection and what risks disconnection.

Over time, these signals quietly shape how we believe we need to behave in order to stay safe and connected.

And those early patterns don't stay in childhood. They shape how we show up in relationships, respond to stress, set boundaries, and speak to ourselves as adults. These early lessons often become the operating system behind our triggers, patterns, self-talk, and sense of worth.

Think back for a moment:

Was conflict something to avoid? Did your parents shut down, avoid, or explode?

Was rest valued, or was performance a badge of honor?

Were tears welcomed or shamed?

Was sensitivity treated as a gift or a burden?

Patterns modeled in childhood don't simply disappear when we grow up.

If anger was the go-to emotion in your home, you may shut down or yell when overwhelmed, not because you want to, but because it's what your nervous system knows. If a parent self-sacrificed to keep the peace, you may struggle to ask for what you need.

These patterns didn't start with you, but they live inside you now, quietly running the show until you bring them into consciousness.

If you see yourself in any of this, take a big breath. You're not flawed. You adapted. These patterns and beliefs aren't who you are. They're inherited survival scripts.

Once you see the script, you get to decide how the story continues.

From these early lessons, we didn't just form beliefs. We learned how to *be* in order to stay safe and connected.

How We Adapted: The Roles We Learned to Play to Feel Safe

If generational wounds are the emotional landscape we inherited, then our learned behaviors are the maps we drew to navigate that terrain.

To stay connected, we adapted.

We became the good child. The strong one. The helper. The achiever. The one who didn't rock the boat.

We learned to be agreeable, capable, easy, because belonging felt safer than risking disconnection.

We learned how to shape-shift for connection, often at the cost of ourselves. If affection was withheld or conditional, you may have learned to earn love through achievement or perfection. If conflict felt unsafe, you may have become the peacemaker. If emotions were dismissed, you may have learned to hide your sensitivity or carry your struggles alone. If the emotional atmosphere in your home felt unpredictable, you may have become the caretaker, constantly scanning the room and managing everyone else's feelings before your own.

These were brilliant adaptive strategies your inner child used to stay safe. At the time, these roles helped you belong. But over time, they can quietly distance you from your authentic self.

The good news? What's learned can be unlearned.

When you care for your inner child, you stop confusing who you *became* with who you *are*.

The Birth of the Inner Critic: How Early Patterns Became Our Inner Voice

The critical voice in your head, the one that says you're not enough, too much, or unworthy isn't actually your voice. The Itty Bitty Shitty Committee is an echo of what you learned, born out of old wounds.

How we were spoken to becomes how we speak to ourselves. How we were treated in our hardest moments becomes how we treat ourselves today.

Think back:

How did your caregivers respond *to you* when you struggled? Did they dismiss, avoid, shame, or explode?

What parts of you brought connection and what parts created distance?

So many of us swore we'd never be like our parents, only to catch ourselves saying the same words or reenacting the same patterns without meaning to. Until we pause and examine these inherited behaviors, they quietly shape how we see ourselves and what we believe we deserve.

Healing begins when we stop punishing ourselves for protective adaptations that once kept us safe. This is the heart of reparenting: To unlearn what love is *not* so we can embrace what love truly *is*.

Unlearning isn't about erasing the past. Unlearning is remembering. Peeling back the layers of protection or shame and returning to the sacred child you've always been.

What was modeled for us became the map. The way conflict, success, love, and even self-worth were expressed or withheld. And unless we bring this map into awareness, we keep following it without realizing we have another choice.

But here's the beauty: You get to keep what worked. And what was passed down can be put down. You do not have to carry what isn't yours.

When we heal ourselves, we don't just change our own lives. We change the generations before us and the ones that follow. We become conscious. We break cycles. We become the safe, loving presence we always needed.

Correct vs. Connect: When Behavior Matters More Than Feelings

Many of us grew up believing our behavior defined us. If we were "good," we were praised and accepted. If we misbehaved, we were scolded, silenced, or shamed. Without meaning to, our parents, often doing the best they could, focused more on our actions than on the emotions underneath.

Clinical psychologist and parenting expert Dr. Becky Kennedy, founder of *Good Inside*, teaches that most of us were raised with "behavior-based" parenting where the focus was on correcting or rewarding behavior instead of recognizing the emotion underneath. If we were upset, anxious, or frustrated, the response wasn't about helping us understand what we were feeling. It was about making the feeling go away.

Parents, often overwhelmed by their own discomfort, tried to control the behavior rather than becoming curious about the emotions beneath it.

Correct instead of connect.

Discipline instead of discuss.

Stop it instead of understand it.

Children are raw emotion, living fully in the present. Their rage, their sadness, their wildness, their sensitivity are often the exact parts of the parent that were once rejected or never given permission to feel. Children can be incredibly triggering for adults who never learned how to process their own emotions. So when a child's feelings made a parent uncomfortable, the instinct was to stop or control the behavior to soothe the parent's discomfort rather than helping the child feel seen.

Of course, guiding a child's behavior is part of parenting. Children need boundaries, structure, and support as they learn how to socialize and navigate the world. But when behavior is corrected without first acknowledging the feeling underneath, the child learns that the emotion itself is the problem. When feelings are met with *reaction* instead of *validation*, big emotions can begin to feel dangerous because they risk disconnection or shame. Love can start to feel conditional.

Very early on, we learned that we were seen as "good" when we were easy and compliant and "difficult" when we were emotional and willful. But in reality, a struggling child with big feelings isn't bad. They are overwhelmed. Dr. Becky reminds us, "Children are not giving you a hard time; they are having a hard time."

When we've been conditioned to see emotions as problems to fix instead of invitations to *connect*, it's easy to fall into *reaction* instead of *reflection*. Behavior is simply a window into a child's unmet needs, not a reflection of their worth.

> *Behavior is simply a window into a child's unmet needs, not a reflection of their worth.*

But when children are met with control instead of compassion, they internalize the message:

This feeling is bad.

I shouldn't feel this.

I am bad.

That belief doesn't disappear when we grow up. We carry it into adulthood, reacting to our emotions the same way our caregivers once did: minimizing, ignoring, judging ourselves, or trying to outrun what we feel.

If sadness once led to disconnection, we learned to push it down.

If anger brought punishment, we learned to hide it.

If sensitivity was invalidated, we restrained it.

But those feelings never really went away. We never stopped feeling. We just stopped expressing.

I see this in my clients all the time. One woman struggled with lifelong anxiety. She had a deeply loving childhood, but her big emotions made her mother uncomfortable. Whenever she expressed fear or nervousness, her mom would say, "Don't worry. There's nothing to be afraid of. Just be happy." Her mom meant well. But what she internalized was clear: *You shouldn't feel this. This feeling is wrong. You are wrong for feeling it.*

As an adult, she began to feel anxious about feeling anxious. And the cycle deepened.

This is how the Itty Bitty Shitty Committee finds its voice. It grows out of early messages that your feelings were too much, too inconvenient, or simply wrong. The critic in your head isn't a bully you were born with. It is the echo of all the times your emotions were corrected instead of connected with.

> *We never stopped feeling—we just stopped expressing.*

The Gap: What We Needed and Didn't Receive

By now, you can probably see how our caregivers' emotional patterns shaped the voice inside us. But there's another layer, one many of us have felt in our bones long before we ever had the words for it.

Our parents may have shown up in practical ways such as packing lunches or cheering in the stands, but emotional presence is something else entirely.

What was missing wasn't love. It was emotional attunement. Someone who could be present and stay with us in all of our feelings. Not fix them. Not rush them away. Simply *be* with us. Sturdy, safe, and still loving us in the middle of our big, messy human emotions.

Most parents were never taught how to be with their own feelings, let alone someone else's. This isn't a failure of character. It's often simply how humans learn to cope when emotions feel too big to navigate.

Sometimes when adults were never taught how to understand or regulate their own emotions, those feelings can become overwhelming. If they weren't allowed to feel anger, sadness, fear, or grief, our big emotions could feel unsettling or hard to hold. They may have shut down, lashed out, or tried to control what felt too big, not because we were wrong, but because they had never learned how to be with their own feelings.

When a parent struggles to sit with their *own* discomfort, they often struggle to sit with *ours*. They may have loved us deeply, but they didn't always know how to stay present with the emotions we were feeling.

Psychologists sometimes refer to this pattern as *emotionally immature parenting*. It can look like a parent becoming overwhelmed by their emotions, numbing through busyness, checking out, or treating feelings as inconvenient. The specifics differ, but the impact is similar. The child learns to manage the parent and suppress their own emotions, rather than being emotionally met in the moment.

None of this means our parents didn't care. It means they didn't have the capacity to give what they were never given. That's where the gap forms: the distance between what we *longed for* and what *we received*.

This is what many psychologists call the *mother–father wound*: the ache of emotional needs that went unseen, unheld, or misunderstood.

And this wound rarely forms in one dramatic moment. It forms in a thousand quiet ones:

Moments when you were praised for complying.

Corrected for questioning.

Shamed for crying.

When your sensitivity or emotions were called "too much."

When your needs were treated as inconvenient.

When you may have learned to take care of others before others took care of your needs.

To survive, you traded authenticity for approval. And that's the birthplace of self-doubt.

As an Asian American daughter of an immigrant mother, I learned to be easy, good, and agreeable. Many Asian cultures place a deep value on respect, harmony, and success. These values carry wisdom and strength, but they can also shape how emotions are expressed and quietly suppressed.

My grandmother embodied the traditional role of the selfless Vietnamese mother. She gave endlessly, rarely complained, and carried herself with quiet endurance. My mom's path was different. She was bold and independent. She moved to America, married outside her culture, and believed deeply in women's independence and freedom.

Yet even with those progressive values, some of the older cultural expectations around respect, success, and obedience still lived quietly in the background.

My mom loved me deeply, and like many parents, conflict could feel uncomfortable for her. If I expressed frustration, it was often seen as disrespectful. Independence sometimes felt like rebellion. Big emotions were often met with an attempt to fix the problem or move past them quickly.

She wanted me to be confident, but at times my boldness challenged the expectations she carried. Slowly, my spark softened, and I learned to tone myself down.

I began to wonder if parts of me were too much.

Over time, beliefs like these quietly begin to form:

I am lovable when I'm happy.

I am accepted when I'm good.

I am worthy when I perform.

When this gap goes unhealed, it becomes the root of our people pleasing, perfectionism, shrinking, and over functioning.

A child who is guided through her emotions learns to trust herself.

A child who feels shamed for her emotions can begin to abandon herself.

It's hard to grow into a confident adult if your fire was once shamed into silence.

But these beliefs were never your identity. They were echoes of someone else's pain.

But echoes fade.

Stories can be rewritten.

The gap can be healed through care.

We can learn to reparent ourselves and become the safe, loving presence we always needed. Healing doesn't mean rejecting our parents. It means reconnecting with ourselves and seeing the innocence in everyone involved.

A child who is guided through her emotions learns to trust herself. A child who feels shamed for her emotions can begin to abandon herself.

This work asks us to care for our own hearts while holding compassion for the hearts that raised us. When we begin to see ourselves with tenderness, our entire lens softens.

When we give ourselves what we were missing and stop outsourcing our worth, we stop waiting for someone else to finally love us the way we've always longed to be loved.

The gap is not the end of your story.

It is where healing begins.

And as you learn to care for the child within, remember:

You are safe now.

Grieve What Wasn't Given: Making Space for What You Needed

Before we move into the self-love tool of Care, let's pause for something tender: grief. This is bold, brave work you are doing.

Healing begins when we allow ourselves to acknowledge what we needed and didn't receive. This isn't about blaming your caregivers. It's about giving your heart the dignity of naming its own ache.

Grief is a gateway. When you let yourself feel the sadness, the unmet needs, the loneliness, you validate your own experience. You honor the child in you who deserved more safety, more tenderness, more presence.

You may be grieving the guidance you longed for and the ways you learned to shrink yourself for love. You may even be grieving the version of you who had to grow up too soon.

Let yourself breathe here.

Let yourself feel.

And when you're ready, offer a gentle release, not for their sake, but for yours. Forgiveness is not about excusing the past. It's about softening what no longer needs to be carried.

Healing has its own rhythm. It meets you gently, right where you are. And with each tender pause, you come home to yourself a little more. That homecoming, that inner steadiness, is the love that will never leave you.

Self-Love Tool #2: Care

For many of us, feeling our emotions, *really feeling them*, wasn't welcomed. Sometimes our feelings were dismissed or punished. Other times, they simply made the people we loved uneasy. And because children are wired for connection, we learned to adapt.

We tucked those parts of ourselves away, trying to be easier to love. We softened, silenced, or overcompensated, just to stay close. We edited ourselves to feel safe or connected.

Without the words, we learned: *When I show this part of me, I lose connection. So I hide it.*

As children, we don't separate behavior from identity.

We don't think, *this feeling is too much.*

We think, *I am too much.*

The story becomes: *If the feeling is "bad," then I must be "bad."*

Remember the castle analogy from earlier in the book? You were born into a magnificent castle, each room holding a radiant, essential part of who you are: the playful, the wild, the tender, the expressive, the sensitive, the bold. But to protect connection, you learned which rooms brought disconnection, so you began to close them off. Those parts didn't vanish, you just learned to hide them behind locked doors.

The truth is, our feelings are not flaws. They are sacred messengers, guiding us back to the parts of ourselves longing to be seen, held, and heard. They whisper: *Please don't turn away. Stay with me. I need you.*

Behavior is not who we are. It's simply a way our emotions try to speak when we don't yet have the language. This is where healing begins—not through correction or control—but through care and presence.

When we stop trying to fix or suppress our feelings, and instead meet them with openness and care, we soften shame and rebuild trust. We begin to remember: *There is nothing wrong with me. I'm allowed to feel it all, because it all is me.*

Why does this matter?

Because when you begin to care for your inner child, you're not just soothing emotions, you're rewiring your entire inner world. The Itty Bitty Shitty Committee is built on old scripts of shame and self-blame. Care interrupts those scripts. It replaces criticism with compassion, fear with safety, and disconnection with belonging...to yourself.

Care is how we begin to reopen the rooms we once locked.

The Cuddle Up Method: Being with Your Feelings

At the heart of caring for our inner child is **The Cuddle Up Method™**, a simple, tender practice that teaches you to stay with yourself instead of abandoning yourself. With it, you meet whatever arises, especially the parts that once felt "too much," with loving attention.

Each time you practice The Cuddle Up Method, you're teaching your nervous system a new message: *I am safe. I am heard. I am enough.*

This is how self-love becomes more than a concept. It becomes something you practice, live, and embody. It's an invitation to return to your castle, to open the doors you once closed and reclaim the wonder, wildness, and wholeness that were always yours.

You can use The Cuddle Up Method anytime, when you feel overwhelmed, triggered, misunderstood, or tender, and also in moments of joy, when your inner child simply wants to be acknowledged and celebrated.

Because when you stay with yourself, you heal. Presence is the practice. Care is the path. And like any relationship, it deepens with devotion.

Step 1: Cuddle Up

Close your eyes. Imagine snuggling up with your inner child. If you have a photo of yourself at age seven or younger, this can help you connect. Gaze into her eyes. Feel her energy, her innocence, her light.

Now, in your mind's eye, draw her close. Let her melt into you. Breathe with her. Be her safe place.

If you don't see her right away, that's okay. She might show up as a feeling, a color, a whisper, or simply a sense of presence. Don't force it. This relationship unfolds slowly, the way trust always does.

Breathe deeply and settle in. Your only job is to stay with her.

Step 2: Ask How She Feels

With gentleness, ask her: "What are you feeling right now?"

Let whatever arises come. Sadness, anger, disappointment, or overwhelm. Let it be what it is. There are no wrong answers.

Feelings aren't problems to fix. They're sacred guides, bridges back to your truth. Just listen without judgment. Emotional regulation isn't about avoiding discomfort. It's about learning to stay with what's uncomfortable, with love.

What if we stopped treating our emotions like problems, and started seeing them as portals to our true self?

Caring for your inner child means giving yourself permission to feel what you couldn't back then. To cry, to yell, to curl up and rest. To play. To be *fully* you.

Feelings aren't problems to fix. They're sacred guides, bridges back to your truth.

When you feel all of your emotions, you heal. Every feeling is a bridge back to you.

Step 3: Validate the Feeling

This is the step where the Itty Bitty Shitty Committee may try to chime in, judging, minimizing, or trying to fix what your inner child shares.

Say to yourself: "Of course I feel this way. It makes sense because…"

"Of course I feel overwhelmed, this is a lot."

"Of course I feel angry, I wasn't treated fairly."

"Of course I feel sad, something I care about is ending."

Validation brings the emotion into the light, where it can be seen, heard, and honored, just like the rest of you. It tells your nervous system: *You are not bad for feeling this.*

Shame thrives in silence, and validation softens it, reminding you: *You are good. This matters.*

Step 4: Listen to Understand

This part may feel tender, but it's also where the magic happens. After you've asked your inner child how she feels, and gently validated her emotions, ask her one more question: "What do you need from me right now to feel safe, supported, and seen?"

Then… listen. *Really listen.*

Quiet the noise of your mind and open your heart to whatever arises.

She might need movement. Or rest. She might want to be held. Or cry. She might ask for stillness, for laughter, for time outside. She might even offer you guidance.

Let her speak, because she knows the way back to your wholeness and joy.

By listening to your inner child, something in your heart will soften, and you'll remember:

You were never bad for feeling.

You never had to shrink, perform, or be perfect.

You were simply human, longing to be heard, seen, and understood.

When you create space to truly listen, your inner child begins to trust you again.

And in that trust, she shows you the way back to yourself. Your emotions are your compass, leading you toward your truest, most liberated self. She knows how to heal. She knows how to play, to live, to feel free. Trust builds when you listen, and she will always show you the way.

Step 5: Offer Care

Now, place your hand on your heart and speak softly to her: "I love you. I see you. I'm here for you. You are safe to feel this."

Let the words land. Breathe them in. Stay here for a few more breaths, soaking in the safety of your own care.

This is what reparenting looks like in real time. You're becoming the loving, conscious presence you once needed, not by fixing yourself, but by remembering your worth was never lost.

You are enough. You matter. You always have.

Let's See This in Real Life

So what does this practice actually look like?

One of my clients, going through a heart-wrenching breakup, heard her inner child whisper during meditation: *Go play. Have fun. You're safe.*

But her mind immediately jumped in: *No. Be productive. Get in the gym and back on those dating apps. Move on already.*

Still, her inner child knew the truth. She didn't need pressure or a plan. She needed presence.

She needed joy, lightness, and her own sweet company so she could feel alive again.

Her inner child was showing her the way home, not to who she should be, but to the joyful, loving woman she had forgotten.

That's the beauty of this work: the truth always returns us to simplicity, innocence, and clarity, just like the child within us. Each time you practice The Cuddle Up Method, you're building trust with the one who needs you most. Every time you stay, she learns it's safe to be fully herself. And the more you listen, the louder her wisdom becomes.

Mothering Myself

One of my hardest experiences as a parent happened on a night when my husband was away. I was on day four of solo parenting. My two-and-a-half-year-old daughter wasn't sleeping at night, and we were both exhausted and running on fumes.

On this particular night, my toddler was caught in an emotional hurricane. She tore around the house, still wet from her bath, and every request to dry off, go potty, or put on pajamas sparked another meltdown.

Finally, I shouted, "My ears hurt from your screaming! This is how you sound when you scream!!"

Okay, who's the child now?

After trying so hard to stay calm and failing miserably, I tried to hug her to repair the emotional damage I'd just caused. But she was too dysregulated to hear me. She slapped me across the face and started hitting me.

I told her if she didn't want to go potty, then she needed to wear a pull-up diaper. That seemed reasonable to me, but to my Tasmanian devil, you'd think I'd asked her to trek across the Sahara barefoot. "No! No! No!" she screamed, kicking as I tried to put it on.

I grabbed her little body and hissed, "Say you're sorry right now!" She kicked me in the gut so hard I dropped her on the carpet and gave her one spank.

She immediately curled into a ball, sobbing, "Owie! Owie! You hurt me, Mommy! Go away!"

Trembling, I ran to my bedroom and locked the door.

A flood of emotions crashed over me. Shame, fear, heartbreak, and the kind of rage that made me afraid of myself. I paced the room, breathing hard and repeating, "Peace begins with me… peace begins with me…" hoping it would calm me down. But instead I fell deeper into it. I punched the air, threw a dramatic karate kick into nothing, and collapsed on the floor in tears. I was well below the line, completely disconnected from who I wanted to be.

Sobbing on the floor, a memory flashed through my mind of my dad demanding that I apologize. Shame washed over me. It was like watching a movie trailer of my own inherited patterns. Like my dad, I'd let my anger become a Category 5 hurricane.

In that moment with my daughter, I could feel myself slipping into the same unconscious patterns: correcting instead of connecting, reacting instead of responding.

At the same time, I could feel another inherited pattern rising in me: the instinct to shut down and escape when emotions became too overwhelming.

And then the truth came with tenderness: my daughter wasn't "too much." She was revealing the parts of myself I'd disowned.

I felt immense remorse. With a few deep breaths, I felt my inner child whisper: *See her. Accept her. She needs you to be the steady shore for her storm.*

My daughter is not bad. She is good and funny and wildly independent and creative. If I could accept her as she is, maybe we wouldn't clash so fiercely.

Then my inner child extended care to me: *Give yourself grace. You're exhausted. She's exhausted. You don't have to show up perfectly. Just show up. Love her. Be with her.*

And suddenly, I saw what I had missed: we were both overextended, and I had not tended to myself. I didn't listen. I tried to control her. When we dip below the line, presence goes offline and our true self feels far away.

Our triggers are our greatest teachers, revealing exactly where love is needed.

When I entered my daughter's bedroom, she was curled in a corner, holding her knees. I reached to touch her leg, but she flinched. So I lay down next to her and whispered, "I'm sorry. I'm so, so sorry. Mommy didn't show up how I wanted to."

> *Our children are living gateways to healing our own childhood pain, so we don't have to pass it on. Repair is how we break the cycle.*

"Mommy, go away. I don't want you!" she snapped.

"I know, baby. Mommy hurt you, and I'm so sorry. I'm going to stay right here with you."

After twenty quiet minutes on the floor, she finally crawled over and snuggled into me, wrapping her little arms around my neck.

"No go, Mommy. Stay," she said.

"I'm not going anywhere. I'm right here for you. Always."

Our children are gateways for healing the pain we once carried. Repair, self-reflection, and care are how we break the cycle.

And the beautiful thing about this inner work is that we can always begin again. No matter how far below the line we fall, peace does begin with us.

We get to choose a different way.

The Gift

Inner child care may feel uncomfortable at first. Not because you're doing it wrong, but simply because you're doing it differently. You're breaking the cycle. You're tending to pain and patterns that were passed down so they finally stop repeating.

With tender Care, you unlearn the old stories that shaped you and release the self-judgment that once kept you small. You meet the places within you that weren't welcomed and whisper: *I'm here now. I'm not leaving.*

This is how you let go of self-doubt and return to self-trust. This is how you create a new kind of love, one that begins inside you and expands outward.

Caring for your inner child means allowing yourself to be the child you weren't allowed to be. It's giving yourself permission to feel deeply, express fully, and play freely.

The gift of inner child work is you remember your worth and reclaim the freedom to be *fully* yourself.

As you practice staying with your big emotions, it becomes easier to honor your needs, boundaries, and desires. The relationship you rebuild with your inner child becomes a devotion to yourself, reminding her and you that you are special, you are loved, you are enough.

This is the magic of reparenting. When you care for yourself with gentleness and truth, you remember your wholeness. You become resilient. And little by little, you feel freer to live as the person you born to be.

And the path forward is simpler than we often think. You simply have to become the one who stays...

With your heart.

With your healing.

With your whole self.

Because you are—and have always been—worthy, wise, and wonderfully whole. And now, you're choosing to believe it.

It helped me to learn that the way we think about "parenting" today is actually quite new. Before Dr. Benjamin Spock's *The Common Sense Book of Baby and Child Care* came out in 1946, the focus was mostly on physical care rather than emotional presence, individuality, or attunement. The word "parenting" didn't even appear in Merriam-Webster until 1958.

When I first learned this, something in me eased. It helped me understand that many of our parents weren't withholding love. They simply weren't taught how to offer emotional presence in the ways we now recognize as essential.

Our parents did the best they could with the tools they had. But now a new way is emerging: mindful reparenting, inner child healing, conscious presence. We are normalizing a new path forward rooted in emotional safety, tenderness, and connection.

And while it can feel like deep work to reparent your inner child, especially if you're also a parent or tending to your parents, I smile imagining the kinder world being born through us.

Dr. Spock began his book with a simple truth that still guides me: "Trust yourself. You know more than you think you do."

From that trust comes a deeper invitation to love not only the tender child within, but also the parts of you that carry shame. Because the true gift of this is simple: you no longer have to hide from who you are. You can stay with yourself and reclaim every part of you.

Integration

The Practice: Daily Devotion Ritual

- Place a photo of your younger self (age seven or under) on your bathroom mirror.
  Each morning, pause, soften, and meet her eyes.
- Ask her: "How are you feeling today, little one?"
  "What do you need from me to feel loved, supported, or celebrated?"
- Honor whatever arises. No fixing. No rushing.
- Offer her a few simple, loving words, such as: "You are safe. You are special. You matter. I love you."
- Then—here's the tender part—look yourself in the mirror and say those same words out loud to your adult self. You might squirm, laugh, avoid your own gaze, or even tear up. That's okay and normal to feel uncomfortable. You're doing something new. That's healing.
- Close with a hand on your heart and remember this truth: You are worthy of love.

Over time, this daily devotion teaches you to treat yourself with the same tenderness you'd offer any sweet, innocent child—because she's still in there. And each time you choose care over criticism, your inner child learns: I am safe. I am worthy. I can be fully me.

Reflection

- What behaviors and patterns were modeled in my home and how are they still living in me today?
- Which parts of me were welcomed, and which parts brought disconnection?
- When I'm triggered or tender, what does my inner child need most from me?

Anahata Chakra

Embracing the Heart's Wisdom

The *Anahata* chakra, the heart chakra, is the center of love, compassion, and connection, both with ourselves and others. Represented by the color green, it is the home of the soul and the gateway to emotional truth.

When this chakra is imbalanced, we may feel lonely, guarded, resentful, jealous, or afraid to let others close. We tighten around our tenderness. We over-give, under-receive, or protect ourselves from disappointment by staying small.

Inner child work reopens the heart. Each time you practice Care by staying with your feelings instead of abandoning yourself, you gently rebalance the Anahata. You begin to trust your own emotions, soften old defenses, and reconnect with the "unstruck sound" of the heart: a quiet, steady knowing that you are safe, loved, and worthy as you are.

When this chakra is aligned, we return to our natural state. We love without losing ourselves. We receive without fear. We show up with presence, patience, and a spaciousness that feels like coming home. The heart is where reparenting truly takes root. The heart is where your inner child finally feels held.

I AM SAFE.
I AM SUPPORTED.
I AM LOVABLE
AND LOVING.
I AM ENOUGH.

CHAPTER 5

COMPASSION

Reclaiming Your Wholeness

"When we bring light into the shadows, we are making room for wounds to transform into healing balm. Balm that we take out into the world and gift as part of our service in the world."

–KATE MURPHY

In the four years since my divorce, I sold my company, moved from California to Florida, started teaching yoga, and for the first time in a long time, felt at home in my own skin. I was getting to know my true self through the inner work of consciously looking within and sitting with it all. New relationships blossomed. But familiar patterns surfaced, too.

I met Jake in my yoga class. He was the epitome of manly. His body was like a dolphin's, sleek and strong. He was also smart, confident, fun, popular, and kind of like Tarzan. He went barefoot most places and bathed in the ocean after surfing. Authentically carefree, Jake had a boyish softness and quiet mystery about him. My ovaries wanted to have his surfer babies.

It took Jake almost a year to ask me out. We were total opposites. His idea of "me time" was summiting a mountain or doing backflips while kiteboarding. My idea of "me time" was lying on my couch with a plate of nachos, watching reruns of *Bridgerton*. Jake dated adventurous tomboys.

I dated men who wore shoes and made dinner reservations. My soft feminine energy was attracted to his fiercely masculine energy, and honestly, that also made me nervous. It was out of my comfort zone. I think we attract opposites because there is a mysterious mirror inside of us that wants to be explored. There was a magnetic attraction between us that neither of us could resist.

After a few months of dating, the spark started to fade, and the real us were left. My flawless facade began to crack, and Jake saw glimpses of my insecurities and neediness. I got glimpses of his selfishness and stubbornness. Relationships trigger the parts in us that are most vulnerable and need attention and healing. In the five months we dated, I watched him slowly fall out of love with me. Well, maybe not love, because he never said he loved me. But I had already started giving him the kind of love I had long denied myself.

Jake went on a business trip, and in the four days he was away, he only texted me once: a photo of a sunrise and the greeting "Morning!" A few days later, I ran into his friend, who told me Jake was in Tallahassee. I thought he was in Kentucky. My heart sank and my Itty Bitty Shitty Committee chimed in: *You don't even know where your boyfriend is. He's probably not calling you because you're not a priority.*

When he got back, Jake left me a voicemail saying he was excited to see me, but he didn't lock down a time. I wanted to see him but didn't want him to know I was desperate. So I made happy-hour plans with some friends to show him how *not desperate* I was. I checked my phone when the evening ended, but there was no call or text from Jake. His aloofness triggered my deep unworthiness wounds and my inner critic confirmed the story I'd believed all my life: *You're not important.*

The next day was Friday, the day Jake and I usually practiced yoga at a cute garage studio. Trying not to be too sensitive and acting like none of this was a big deal, I casually texted him: "Still on for yoga tonight?" He texted back a few hours later: "Can't. Have a triathlon meeting. Come if you want."

I felt like Miranda in the TV show, *Sex and the City* when she realized "that guy was just not that into me." My face felt hot, my eyes swelled, and my heart ached. It felt like my heart was splitting into thousands of pieces. I closed my eyes. Breathe in. Breathe out.

After several minutes of bawling mixed with deep breathing—in the middle of that heartache—something shifted. A faint flooding of warmth filled my heart. It was a foreign feeling, as if my heart was hugging my spirit and rocking me like a baby. This tenderness was my inner knowing.

I had been forcing this relationship, hoping Jake would wake up one day and realize what an amazing, perfect girl I was for him. Maya Angelou has this powerful quote: "When someone shows you who they are, believe them." It wasn't enough to fall in love with the potential of Jake loving me. Potential wouldn't love me 'til death do us part.

I'd been in this codependent, destructive cycle many times before. In the past, I held on, tiptoed around my partner, or molded myself to be the "perfect" girl, hoping he would finally love me. We repeat what we don't repair. Although I was falling in love with Jake, I was ready to break my codependent chase for love. The emotional ride was too volatile for my heart.

Each person we attract reflects what's whole in us and what parts need healing and integration.

This was a pivotal moment. It wasn't about Jake choosing me. It was about *me* choosing me.

After three decades of searching outside myself for love and worthiness, I was still learning the lesson that no money, relationship, accomplishment, or possession would give me the validation I desired. I longed to feel deep connection, care, and love…but it had to come from within me.

I believe our relationships are mirrors. Each person we attract reflects what's whole in us and what parts need healing and integration. The parts of ourselves we've abandoned, denied, or hidden away are our shadows. When we view our relationships through this lens, even the painful ones become invitations: opportunities to learn the lesson we've been avoiding and evolve into the whole, expansive version of ourselves we're here to be.

Our shadows didn't form because something was wrong with us. They formed because something in us was trying to survive and feel connected.

So, I got quiet and sat with the dark parts of me I had voted off the island, my shadows. I allowed these undesirable shadows into the light of my consciousness: Insecure Isabel, Sensitive Sally, Unlovable Ursula, Jealous Jan, and Needy Nancy, key members of my Itty Bitty Shitty Committee. I listened to their worries, and as I sat with these unlovable parts of myself, they eventually grew quiet. Together, we'd found some closure, as a loving whisper assured me I would be okay.

In that moment of sorrow and bitterness, an inner knowing swelled my heart, and I realized: we are all just human beings trying to do the best we can with what we have at the moment. We are all the same souls with the same fears of being unlovable, alone, not enough, and we all have the same desires to feel loved, seen, and significant. When I could see myself through the eyes of compassion, I could also see Jake through the eyes of compassion.

Triggers are teachers if we stay open to their lessons. Although I longed to be with Jake, we were exactly where we were supposed to be. Instead of resentment, I chose to offer us both compassion. For the first time in any romantic relationship, I released my expectation of how he should be and accepted that he was perfect just as he was. And so was I. We just weren't perfect together. At least not then.

Jake agreed to see me before his triathlon meeting. We sat on his bed. I put my hand on his leg, forced a kind smile, and told him, with tears in my eyes: "I'm falling in love with you. But you're not in love with me, and

I want to be wanted. Maybe it's just not the right time, or I'm not the right fit for you. So, I lovingly release you to go find her."

Jake was silent.

In less than five minutes, I was back in my car, driving home. Alone and single.

But I also felt mature, proud, and awake. I vowed that the next person I gave my heart to would make me a priority and love me back.

Turns out, that person was me.

We Repeat What We Don't Repair

Before we dive into our next Self-Love Tool, **Compassion**, I want to remind you that the five self-love tools in this book aren't linear. While Consciousness lays the foundation, each tool is part of your Soul Toolkit, ready for you whenever you need it. It's not a destination or trying to be perfect, but a forever practice of peeling back what is false to reveal what is true.

In the last chapter, we explored inner child healing, the tender act of meeting our big emotions with softness and care. Now we take that tenderness deeper. Because the parts we reject or deny, the ones we feel shame around, don't stay contained in our inner world. They leak into our outer world, shaping our relationships, reactions, and patterns.

These hidden parts are what Carl Jung called the *shadow*, the aspects of ourselves we've disowned. Even when we push them away, they still show up in who we attract, the patterns we repeat, and the habits we can't seem to break. Often, the shadow looks like self-sabotage.

But when we relate to these parts with compassion instead of criticism, we discover something unexpected: **the very places we judge or hide often hold the seeds to our greatest gifts.**

Shadow work is deeply connected to inner child healing. Most of our shadows—the parts of us that learned shame, rejection, or fear and hid them away in order to belong—were born from the wounded child. Rather than meeting these parts with criticism or compliance, through compassion we stop disowning our parts and begin to re-member who we are.

You might be thinking, *But I don't want to look at these dark parts of me that make me feel shame.* I get it.

But the truth is this: We repeat what we don't repair.

Growth isn't linear. It's a spiral.

And what we avoid always finds a way to rise, especially when life starts to get good.

Our shadows aren't here to punish us. They're here to free us. If we don't learn the lesson they're pointing to, we repeat the pattern.

We often find ourselves in the same pattern, attracting the same kind of partner, reacting the same way, repeating the same behavior. We circle back again and again, wondering why life keeps bringing us the same lesson.

But what's really happening is that life is inviting us deeper.

A spiral moves up and down, in and out, mirroring the rhythm of life itself.

The spiral invites us to descend into the dark to integrate, heal, or repair something within ourselves so we can rise into a fuller expression of who we are. It might ask us to contract and go inward to tend to what lies beneath the surface so we can expand again more fully.

If you're paying attention and meeting your shadows with compassion, each turn of the spiral brings you closer to your wholeness and the depth of who you truly are.

As we learn the lesson and integrate it, we may return to the same pattern, but can see it with a new perspective and wiser eyes.

That's the nature of the spiral. It's a continual rhythm of descent and rising, contracting and expanding, learning and evolving.

If you're paying attention and meeting your shadows with compassion, each turn of the spiral brings you closer to your wholeness and the depth of who you truly are.

Think about every movie or story you've ever loved. Why do we root for the heroine?

Because she goes through something difficult. A breakup. A loss. A reckoning.

She faces her own darkness, and in doing so discovers her power.

That's what shadow work offers us. It doesn't bypass the hard parts. It transforms them into the very source of our strength.

This chapter is your invitation to meet the parts of yourself you've exiled. Not to fix them. Not to shame them. But to recognize your shadows as portals to your radiance, your worthiness, and the wholeness that's been there all along.

We may want an easy, breezy life, but it's often the dark moments that shape us.

When we meet our shadows with compassion, the darkness doesn't consume us—it reveals us.

Our shadows illuminate the path to our gifts.

So now that we've explored why shadows matter, let's look at what a shadow actually is and how to begin setting ourselves free.

What Is a Shadow?

From the time we are young, we begin slicing off parts of our 360-degree personality that feel shameful, messy, too much, or not enough. These splintered-off pieces don't disappear. They become our shadows: the parts of ourselves we've rejected, buried, or tried to outrun. Because we feel ashamed, we push them underground.

But what we suppress doesn't go away. These parts operate in the background, surfacing in sabotaging ways. They show up in our reactions, relationships, and habits, especially when stress, fear, or vulnerability hits.

It might look like picking a fight in the middle of a romantic weekend. Raiding the pantry when you're so close to your goal weight. Longing for financial freedom but overspending anyway. Or staying stuck researching a dream instead of taking the first step.

These are our shadows at work—the parts of us that hit self-destruct just as we're about to break through. When they go unacknowledged, they find new ways to make themselves known.

Our shadows aren't here to ruin your life. They're invitations calling you to turn toward the parts of yourself you once banished and bring them back home.

How to Recognize a Shadow

There are four main places shadows tend to hide: in **shame**, in our **triggers**, in **projection**, and in the **patterns** we repeat. Once you can spot them, you can begin meeting them with compassion and finally open the door to real healing and wholeness.

You don't need to master all of this at once. Allow these practices to be mirrors, not mandates. Take what resonates, and move at the pace your nervous system can hold.

Okay, are you ready? Take a deep, loving breath. I'm right here with you, so let's do this together.

What parts of me bring up shame?

Let's start by reflecting:

- What parts of me feel hard to accept?
- What would be the worst thing someone could say about me: the thing that would make me shut down or feel ashamed?

Maybe it's jealousy. Rage. Neediness. Competitiveness with other women. Control. Laziness. Stubbornness.

We all have parts of ourselves we'd rather not see: the procrastinator, the bad mom, the gossip, the know-it-all, the pessimist, the victim, the mean girl. I know these words sting, but that's why they matter because they show us where shame still lives.

Think back to earlier in the book when we brought awareness to the voice of your Itty Bitty Shitty Committee, the one that whispers:

You're a loser.

You're incapable.

You're too old.

You're stupid.

These aren't just cruel thoughts. They're your shadow parts, the pieces you've rejected or tried to hide.

Someone might feel fine being called messy, but the word lazy cuts deep. You might admit you're a bit controlling, but feel humiliated if someone called you manipulative. Here's the key: if a word triggers you—making you shrink or get defensive—that's likely a repressed shadow. If you can name a trait neutrally or with curiosity, then you've most likely already made peace with that part of you.

Okay, let's take a moment of pause here. This is BIG work. So, take a few deep breaths and place your hands over your heart. Inhale gently... and exhale slowly.

This is deep, freaking hard work. The *real* kind! It takes massive courage to turn the mirror inward and meet the parts you've been avoiding. But shadow work isn't here to shame you more. It's here to illuminate what's been quietly operating in the background and offer a new way of seeing yourself.

Because these parts you're ashamed of and exiled? They're still there waiting to be welcomed. And when you meet them with love, they don't have to fight for your attention anymore. Through compassion they can soften, and you can begin to feel whole and free.

What Triggers You

Another way to uncover your shadow is to notice what activates you in others. What qualities get under your skin?

It might be the mom on Instagram making homemade sourdough with her perfect top knot, triggering the part of you that feels like you're failing at motherhood.

Or the overly emotional friend reminding you of how you were never allowed to cry without being told to toughen up.

Or you keep over-giving, just like the self-sacrificing parent you swore you wouldn't become because being needed feels safer than needing others.

Ask yourself:

- What do I judge or criticize in others that might reflect something I've disowned in myself?

The qualities we can't stand in others often point to something unresolved in us; not because we're bad, but because those parts want to be seen, reclaimed, and loved. Our triggers are sacred clues. They don't always feel good, but they reveal where something in us still feels tender or unseen.

If we follow them with compassion, they lead us back to our true self.

What You Project Onto Others

Another way we find our shadows is by noticing where we project our own disowned parts onto someone else. This is the classic case of the person who doesn't trust their partner, when they're actually the one hiding something.

It can sound like: She's so angry. He's so dramatic. I just can't deal with people like that.

Projection can be subtle. Maybe you show you care by micromanaging or constantly worrying about someone, but under the surface, your controlling shadow is gripping tight, afraid of what might happen if you let go.

Maybe you complain about a co-worker being "too much," but there's a part of you that secretly longs to be bold, unapologetic, and fully expressed.

Or maybe you call your partner selfish because he goes to the gym and takes time for himself, while you're stewing in resentment, craving the care you no longer give yourself.

Projection is sneaky. It often reveals the parts of us we've buried to survive. But what we push away in ourselves will always find a way to show up, often reflected in the people around us.

Ask yourself:

- What am I seeing in others that I might be avoiding in myself?
- What activates me because it also exists in me, too?

Projection isn't something to judge. It's something to get curious about. Because often, what we criticize in others is actually a sacred part of us asking to be seen and accepted.

If you're feeling tender or exposed right now, pause. This work isn't about fixing yourself; it's about seeing your *whole self* with more honesty and acceptance and less fear and rejection.

The Patterns You Repeat

The final way to discover your shadows is to look at the patterns you can't seem to shake.

Ask yourself:

- Where do I keep getting stuck, even though I "know better?"
- What patterns or beliefs keep sabotaging what I truly want?

Perhaps you want to attract a romantic partner who is emotionally mature and all in, but keep accepting the partner who needs fixing.

Maybe you crave success, but can't stop playing small or undercharging because receiving still feels unsafe.

Maybe you finally have a free hour to yourself, but instead of resting or doing something that nourishes you, you rage-clean the kitchen.

Maybe you want to grow and heal, but it's never the "right" time to make that therapy appointment.

These aren't just bad habits. They're shadow coping strategies, parts of you trying to keep you safe in your old patterns and comfort zone. But in their protection, they also keep you small.

Your shadows are like arrows pointing you back to the parts of you that still feel unworthy, unloved, or unsafe. Awareness helps you see the pattern. Compassion softens it. And from there, choice becomes possible.

A Reframe

And if the word "shadow" feels confusing or even a little edgy, here's another way to see it. Therapies like Internal Family Systems (IFS) call these "parts" of us, different inner voices or roles we developed to help us survive. Some parts protect, some carry pain, and some hold the needs we never had met.

None of these parts are broken or bad. They simply never got the safety or care they needed. When ignored, they act out, not because they're evil or wrong, but because they're desperate to be seen and held.

Your shadows aren't here to expose you. They're here to free you.

Shadow work and parts work are different ways of pointing toward the same sacred truth: reclaiming all of who you are. You are not broken. You're multifaceted. Your true self is already whole and enough. Every part of you is a thread in the tapestry of who you're becoming.

Both shadow work and parts work are invitations to sit with the pieces of yourself you've exiled, not with shame or blame, but with radical compassion. To listen to them. To understand them. To integrate them. To unlock a door you once shut and whisper:

You can come back now.

I see you.

I'm not afraid of you anymore.

To say: You belong here too.

Your shadows aren't here to expose you. They're here to free you.

Fat Kid Freddy

Let me tell you about one of my parts. Beyoncé has her alter ego, Sasha Fierce. I have Fat Kid Freddy.

I know, that name is harsh! But that's how my shame talks. Our shadows don't hold back, and the Itty Bitty Shitty Committee isn't kind. It shames with ruthless precision.

Freddy is my fried-food-loving, mac-and-cheese-obsessed alter ego. He shows up when I'm overwhelmed, exhausted, or emotionally maxed out. When he's driving the bus, I'm not in control—he is. And Freddy? He believes food is safety. Food is comfort. Food is love.

He's got a full-blown scarcity mindset. *If I don't eat those French fries right now, I'll never get the chance again!* So, I might as well eat. it. all. Just last week, I was at Whole Foods ordering a green juice (look at me, making good choices!), then I saw the donuts next to the juice bar. *Why though, why?!* Without thinking, I grabbed a maple bar. Then beelined past the salad bar and straight to the hot bar, where I filled a box with mashed potatoes, gravy, and mac and cheese. I scarfed it all down in the car and saved the juice for later, like some sort of sad wellness punchline.

Did I learn my lesson? No. As soon as my Itty Bitty Shitty Committee started screaming that I'd "ruined my day," I gave up and ended the night eating a slice of chocolate cake in the garage. At 8 p.m. By myself. In the dark

That's the shadow. That's Fat Kid Freddy in full effect.

I sort of laugh about him, but the spiral that follows isn't funny: shame, guilt, and a quiet voice that says, "You're indulgent and weak. You're reckless and out of control. You're never going to change." My critic doesn't hold back, and maybe yours doesn't either.

But my Freddy isn't the enemy. He's the part of me that panics when I'm feeling uncomfortable emotions I don't want to feel. He's the one who reaches for food when what I really need is comfort, safety, and reassurance. He reaches for carbs, when really, he craves care.

Freddy keeps showing up in my sabotaging patterns because, like so many of our shadows, he's trying to protect me in the only way he learned early on. Emotional eating feels safer than emotional feeling.

But when I meet my shadow with compassion instead of judgment, something shifts. I can be with the deeper feelings underneath the cravings. The ones that say:

"I'm afraid to feel this."

"I don't know how to handle this."

"This feels like too much."

Or even, "This situation feels too good, so I have to sabotage it to feel comfortable again."

I used to stay stuck in that shame story for days. But now, when I can be conscious of the shadow, I get to choose compassion instead. When I reach for my steady heart instead of the snack drawer, there's always something tender underneath. A part of me wants to know: *Will I be okay?*

It's only when I meet Fat Kid Freddy with compassion that I can see what's really going on. The part of me that feels out of control is just overwhelmed by emotions I don't yet know how to hold.

And when I pause and offer compassion instead of punishment, a gift always rises to the surface, some quiet truth that's been there all along, waiting for me to slow down and listen. Nothing outside can comfort me the way my Soul and True Self can. I can be the steady shore for my big, scary emotions, and remember: *I will be okay when I can be with all of myself.*

Unmask Shame

Now, maybe your "Freddy" doesn't binge food. Maybe she scrolls Instagram, pours another glass of wine, shops, overworks, or rage-cleans the house. While our coping mechanisms may be different, our shadows leave the same mark: shame.

We all have those parts we'd rather not see. The ones that bring up shame or make us feel ashamed. But these aren't problems to punish; they're parts to be present with. They act out not to sabotage you, but to get your attention so they can finally rest and return to harmony within you.

Here's what usually happens: when a part of you feels shame, the instinct is to cover it up. So you put on a mask.

Maybe you became the good girl who swallows her needs.

The woman who hides her depth because she fears, *If he knew the real me, he'd leave.*

Or the achiever who performs her way into belonging and feeling validated.

These masks start as protection from feeling vulnerable, exposed, or ashamed. But the cost is that each mask you put on is a tiny step away from your own expansive soul.

So you dim. You silence your voice. You shrink to fit into spaces where your fullness won't fit. You trade authenticity for approval. You think you're avoiding rejection, but really, you're rejecting yourself.

Here's the invitation: you don't have to keep hiding or ignoring. You can begin now by noticing where you've been performing, naming the places you've been shrinking, and letting yourself be seen...even when it feels terrifying.

Because every mask you drop opens a door back to your magnificent castle. And every shadow you reclaim brings you closer to the home you've been searching for all along—your true self.

And it's not just your pain hiding behind those masks. Your brilliance has been hiding there too.

Light Shadows

It's not just our "negative" or dark parts we exile. We also tuck away our brilliance. These are our light shadows—the radiant, powerful, "positive" qualities we dimmed to belong.

Your wildness. Your bigness. Your sensuality. Your creativity. Your intelligence. Your beauty. Your spirituality. All those luminous parts of you that once lit up a room, until someone called them "too much." And so, you shrank.

Maybe someone said your joy was annoying. Your confidence arrogant. Your sensuality inappropriate. Your fire too wild. So you stayed small to stay connected. You stopped trusting your shine. And in doing so, you disconnected from your magic.

Because when you dim your light, you deny your power. You abandon the very gifts you're here to share.

Your light shadows aren't gone. They're still alive inside you, flickering under the surface, waiting for permission to be seen and set free.

When you dim your light, you deny your power. You abandon the very gifts you're here to share.

Take a moment and reflect: what parts of your light have you been taught to hide or dismiss, and how might your life change if you reclaimed them and let them shine?

The Wheel of Wholeness: Reclaiming Your Parts

Both dark and light shadows aren't bad. They're just unclaimed. And your shadows will keep showing up, in your habits, your relationships, and your inner dialogue, to invite you back to your fullest self. Because once your shadows are seen, they don't have to scream. And when you've healed and accepted a shadow, you can also access its counterpart. Often, the shadow you fear most is guarding the light you've been searching for. We need both to feel balanced, whole, and free.

So the question is: are you willing to open and reclaim all of your unique parts? To meet all of yourself with honesty, presence, and love...to truly accept and see *all* of yourself.

This is the sacred homecoming of collecting your fragments—your messy, brilliant, beautiful parts—and bringing them back into the light through compassion, so you can finally feel whole and free in your truest self.

And once you begin claiming these parts, something shifts. You start seeing your shadows less as enemies and more as guides, leading you back to your wholeness, wisdom, and worthiness that have been within you all along.

Let me share how this unfolded for me in one of the rawest, most pivotal moments of my own healing...

Finding Wholeness

I wasn't going to share this story. Even the people closest to me, my mom and dad, my best friends, have never heard it. I've written it, scrapped it, and rewritten it more times than I can count, but I finally worked up the courage to share it because too many women carry shame in silence, and I don't want you to feel like you're the only one.

So I'm taking off the mask to show you my vulnerable heart and give you permission to meet your heart too. Whatever shame you're carrying, I want you to know this: **You're not alone.**

Okay. Deep breath. Here goes...

My first boyfriend in high school left a wound I carried for years. I was sixteen, and he was five years older, drinking, smoking pot, already living in a world I thought was cool and grown-up. I was innocent and naïve and mistook his attention for love.

I didn't learn about it until later, but he and his friends had a cruel "club" they bragged about: *Turning Virgins into Whores.* To their guy friends it was a joke, but to young girls like me they pretended we were special while quietly manipulating us into things we didn't want to do.

I stayed with him for over a year, convincing myself he cared. But a piece of me—my purity, my innocence—felt stolen. That wound planted one of the shadows I carried the longest: the fear that I was ruined, dirty, not good enough.

Years later, at my first inner child and shadow work retreat led by Jana Wilson, I sat in a circle with a group of strangers and had no idea my life was about to split open.

Jana created a safe, loving container, a space where every part of us was allowed to be witnessed without judgment. Then she guided us through an exercise that would change everything for me.

We each drew a giant circle on paper to represent our 360-degree personality. On one side, we wrote the dark qualities we'd rather not admit, the parts we judge as "bad" or shameful. On the opposite side, we wrote their counterparts, the light qualities we longed to claim but couldn't.

Each pair became a spoke in the wheel, because for every dark shadow there is its counterpart, and together they make up just a sliver of our whole self.

I'm going to share the exact words I wrote that day, even though they still make my chest tighten, because it's important to understand how shame hides in all of us.

I started listing: controlling, needy, insecure, jealous, selfish. Those were easy enough.

Then I stared at the page, my stomach churning. Two words burned like fire: *failure* and *slut.*

I wanted to scurry out of there. My hand shook as I wrote them anyway, the paper crinkling under my fingers.

When it was my turn to share, my voice shook.

"I'm a failure. I'm a slut."

The room went silent.

As part of the exercise, under Jana's loving guidance, the whole group repeated my words back to me. I thought I might throw up.

But they said it anyway.

"You're a failure. You're a slut."

Again.

And again.

Until the tears broke. I collapsed into the grief of how long I'd been carrying that shame.

Then Jana looked at me with so much love and said, "Now say this: I am pure."

I snorted out loud. *Pure? Me?*

It felt ridiculous, like a word that belonged to someone else. But I rolled my eyes and said it reluctantly. "I am pure."

The group echoed back, "You are pure."

I said it again.

They repeated it again.

Over and over.

Louder.

With more certainty.

Until something cracked open and the tears came harder. Not from shame this time, but from love.

I could feel it, the part of me I had abandoned that carried my light. The truth that purity and specialness still lived inside me waiting to be reclaimed.

I closed my eyes and breathed in both the *slut* and my *purity*.

That was the breakthrough. Not just owning the dark shadow, but embracing its counterpart. Because sometimes the light is harder to claim than the dark.

Sometimes it's easier to believe the worst about ourselves than to accept the truth of our brilliance.

That day I realized wholeness isn't about choosing one side of the circle over the other. It's about holding both:

The slut and the pure girl.

The failure and the woman who is special and worthy.

The dark and the light.

Each bears gifts. All of it belongs.

Maybe your shame words aren't mine, but every woman carries a part of herself that still brings up shame.

And that's where the real healing begins, when we stop exiling our parts and start inviting them back to ourselves through compassion.

Self-Love Tool #3: Compassion

When we bring compassion to our dark shadows instead of condemnation, something sacred happens: we let go of the pressure to be perfect, perform, and the shame we've been carrying in our wounds to see ourselves clearly, hold ourselves tenderly, and finally feel like we belong to ourselves.

Compassion is welcoming every part of you home. Through a process I call **Name It, Tame It, Claim It,** we learn to befriend the pieces we've pushed away. It's simple and powerful, and will change your life.

The Persian poet Rumi offers this reminder in his poem *The Guest House*:

The dark thought, the shame, the malice
meet them at the door laughing

and invite them in...
Be grateful for whoever comes...
because each has been sent as a guide.

What if your shame wasn't an enemy but a guide?

What if every trigger was a treasure guiding you to your fullest, freest self?

When we stop running from ourselves, life becomes our greatest classroom. Every uninvited guest, especially the darkest shadows, holds a gift if we're willing to listen. Even the parts we once tried to muzzle carry the wisdom we've been searching for. Instead of being the victim of our patterns, we become the author of our story.

So how do we do this in real life, without getting swallowed by shame? Here's the practice I use with myself and my clients. Think of it as your map back to yourself: Name It, Tame It, Claim It.

Name It

Have you ever noticed that it's easier to see someone else's patterns than your own? Or how you can give the best advice to a friend but totally ignore it in your own life? It's because we need space to see ourselves clearly. Our shadows live so close to us, they *feel* like us.

Naming brings you back to the present moment and creates space. It moves the shadow from "me" to "something I'm experiencing." Suddenly, instead of drowning in shame, you're observing the pattern with presence, rather than conditioning. Consciousness shifts your perspective to see something new. Naming softens the charge. It keeps you from becoming the shame and allows you to stay in relationship with yourself.

It's like when you help a toddler name their feelings: "You're mad. Mad. Mad." The moment the emotion has a name, the child feels safer. The same is true for us.

So let's begin. Grab a piece of paper and draw a big circle. On the left, write down the qualities you'd hate for someone to call you:

Incapable. Insecure. Stupid.

Jealous. Lazy. Selfish.

Needy. A failure. A bitch.

If a word triggers you, circle it. That's a shadow asking for your attention.

Now, on the right, write its opposite light, "positive" quality that lives on the other side of that same energy. You may also write other light qualities that feel hard to own. These are also your shadows. Now, connect the opposing qualities with a line, like spokes on a wheel:

- Controlling → Organized and caring
- Selfish → Giving
- Lazy → Restful and receptive
- Helpless → Empowered

This is your **Wheel of Wholeness**, a reminder that you're not just *one* thing. You carry *multitudes*. Often the very thing we avoid is the path to our gifts. Compassion allows us to accept both the dark and the light, and become free.

Want to make it lighter? Give your shadows names: Angry Agnes, Jealous Jan, Fearful Fran. Humor helps soften the heaviness of this work. When you name a shadow, the shame loosens its grip. Because what we name, we can finally work with. And if that feels weird, simply see this as a wounded part of you asking for compassion.

Tame It

Carl Jung said, "Until you make the unconscious conscious, it will direct your life and you will call it fate."

What we refuse to recognize runs our lives. What we welcome begins to heal. Taming a shadow is simply bringing it loving attention, not with control or shame, but with compassion. Think of it as three invitations: **listen without judgment, forgive without resentment,** and **accept without conditions.**

1. Listen without judgment

When a shadow flares—anger, jealousy, insecurity, anxiety, or yes, cake in the garage at 8 p.m. (ahem)—pause. Breathe. And listen. Often our shadows are just wounded younger parts of us who need to be heard.

Emotions are like a teapot: when you ignore the pressure, the steam finds a way out sideways. But when you gently lift the lid, you release what's building inside. Compassion lets the emotion be felt instead of feared.

Try this 60-second, mini-practice to feel your feelings:

- Place your hand on heart, hand on belly.
- Take slow breaths.
- Say to your emotion: "I see you. I hear you. I'm here."
- Ask the emotion: "What are you afraid of? What do you need?"
- Let yourself breathe and just be with the feeling, without judgment or fixing. Be with it as it is, and allow your steady breath to steady the fiery pull.

2. Forgive without resentment

Forgiveness isn't about approving behavior; it's about loosening shame's grip. The Hawaiian healing practice *Ho'oponopono* offers a simple, but powerful prayer for softening the heart:

I'm sorry.
Please forgive me.
Thank you.
I love you.

Repeat it silently, directing the words toward yourself or someone else, until you feel even the smallest shift.

3. Accept without conditions

Acceptance doesn't mean you adore your anxiety or celebrate your rage. It means letting emotions exist without making them wrong. Some of the parts we shame—rage, control, selfishness—have actually been trying to protect us.

When we accept a part of ourselves, we stop making it wrong. We recognize it as one voice inside a much bigger, wiser whole. This is where compassion disarms the inner war.

Claim It

This is where the work turns into transformation. Claiming means taking radical ownership of your whole self, not just the parts you like. It sounds like: *This part is me too, and it belongs. It has a seat at the table. And I choose to live in harmony with it.*

> *The very qualities we push away often hold our greatest gifts.*

When you claim your shadow, you integrate it into your wholeness and transform shame. And in doing so, you also reclaim its hidden light. The very qualities we push away often hold our greatest gifts.

For years, I believed that my sensitivity was a liability. When it was out of balance, it showed up as insecurity and neediness, or the opposite, pretending to be aloof and independent like I didn't care (but really cared so much).

The truth? My sensitivity is my superpower.

When I claimed it instead of condemning it, it stopped running the show from the shadows. It came into harmony. And when in balance, my sensitivity makes me empathetic, intuitive, and deeply connected to others. It's the special gift I bring into every healing space with my clients.

This is why claiming matters, because wholeness is power. When you claim a shadow, you stop outsourcing your worth. You stop being the victim of your story, and become the author of it. You step into your most expansive, authentic self.

One of my clients was the ultimate "good girl." The good wife. The good mom. The woman who gave and gave, always with a smile on her face, never asking for anything in return. Anger wasn't in her vocabulary.

When we started exploring her shadows, one word triggered her more than any other: "bitch." Just hearing it made her defensive and upset. Yet beneath that smile lived a quiet rage of being everything for everybody. This rage wasn't bad; it was the flare showing exactly where she'd abandoned herself.

The shadow that triggered her the most, *the bitch*, was actually the gift.

The bitch? She's bold, fierce, and clear. She sets boundaries. She speaks her truth. She's wild and authentically herself. She's free! Sometimes we need to embrace our inner bitch.

The keyword here is *sometimes*. When our shadows are accepted, they find harmony with all aspects of ourselves. For her, the bitch was the antidote to years of people-pleasing. Her rage wasn't her enemy. It was her teacher, whispering, *Stop abandoning yourself. You deserve to choose yourself.*

And when she claimed that shadow and said, "Yes, this too belongs," she reclaimed her light, her freedom, her aliveness, her voice, her fire.

This is the essence of claiming: shadows become sacred guides. Compassion doesn't cancel that part of you; it offers it a seat and a purpose. You integrate all of it, without shame. Both the "bitch" and the "nice girl" can co-exist in balance. And slowly, compassion weaves you whole again.

So let me ask you:

What shadow can you claim now, not as something wrong, but as something wise?

And what gift or teaching has been hiding underneath it?

To take this deeper, choose one shadow that feels triggering from your **Wheel of Wholeness** and walk it through **Name It, Tame It, Claim It** on paper. Just one. Keep it simple. Notice what insights arise when you meet yourself with compassion, when you listen to this part of you with an open ear and an open heart.

What does it want you to know?

What lesson is trying to teach you so you can become more whole within yourself?

Also, notice what it's opposite counter shadow is offering, which often has gifts and guidance for you too.

Claiming is radical ownership saying: *I am remembering and reclaiming all that I am. I am free to be all of me.*

When you name it, tame it, and claim it, your shadows stop running your life from the dark and start guiding you in the light. This is how you rise into your wholeness and reign in your sovereignty.

Relationships Are Mirrors

Our shadows are most clearly activated in our relationships. Nothing exposes our hidden wounds or unhealed patterns like intimacy does. Relationships don't just trigger us—they reveal us. I often like to do a perspective shift: what if your soul didn't send you these heartbreaks and patterns to punish you, but to grow you? To wake up the parts of you that are ready to heal and rise?

Because every person who enters your life is a mirror showing you the wounds you've tucked away and the places you still abandon yourself. Each one arrives for your soul's evolution.

As spiritual author Gary Zukav writes, a spiritual partnership is "a partnership between equals for their spiritual growth." The people we love most aren't here to complete us; they're here to grow us. And in conscious relationships, growth starts as an inside job.

But growth rarely feels comfortable at first. Intimacy shines a light on our darkest corners, exposing the masks we've worn to feel safe. And when intimacy touches an unhealed place, it can feel like heartbreak.

Heartbreak is brutal, yes, but it's also holy. It burns down the roles you played to be loved and reveals what's been waiting underneath. What you hide to keep love, you eventually resent. The longer you swallow your truth to keep the peace, the more invisible you become. When you dim your light so someone will stay close, in the process, you disappear from your own life.

It often sounds like:

If I speak my truth, they'll leave.

If I grow too much, I'll outgrow the relationship.

If I shine too bright, I'll make someone uncomfortable.

So we stay loyal to the version of ourselves that first got love, even when she no longer feels true.

But you don't have to wait for a breakup to reclaim yourself. You can begin now by meeting the truth you've buried, letting yourself be seen even when it scares you, and loving someone without shrinking for them. If a relationship can't hold that, it was never the container for your becoming. Compassion has room for love and boundaries. You can open your heart without abandoning your safety or your truth

And this is where compassion becomes your superpower, because the more you can hold your own shadows, the more space you create for love that's conscious, not conditional.

My relationship with Jake became one of my greatest teachers. It revealed my shadows, showed me where I was still abandoning myself, and gave me the chance to practice speaking my truth with love. Not to fix him. Not to rescue him. But to choose myself while calling in a conscious partnership.

After we broke up, I couldn't seem to escape him. Jake popped up everywhere—at the beach, in the grocery store, even at a yoga class where I was sure he wouldn't be. *Universe, really? I'm trying to move on here.*

For several months the synchronicities kept coming, until finally a four-page letter landed on my porch. Jake poured out his feelings and asked to see me.

We met at our favorite beach. As the sky blushed in shades of tangerine and pomegranate, Jake told me he was falling in love with me but was scared because we were so different.

This time, I wasn't the girl trying to fix him or cling to him. I was rooted in the work I'd been doing of meeting myself with compassion, wholeness, and accepting the parts of me I once rejected. From that place, I could meet him with clarity and softness. I shared what I'd discovered: a soul partnership isn't about sameness or a conflict-free life; it's about growth. Two people committed to their own evolution, walking side by side. Not blaming. Not fixing. Just owning their inner work and loving each other through it.

In the past, we met below the line. His stubbornness triggering my insecurity, my insecurity fueling his withdrawal. We played out old karmas. He'd pull away, I'd cling tighter. But when we stopped seeing each other as the *problem* and started seeing each other as *mirrors*, everything shifted.

Jake had thought, "The more independent I am, the more independent she'll be." But independence without compassion is just isolation.

True love isn't: *You're on your own.*

It's: *I'm working on myself, and you're working on yourself. And even though I know you can swim, if I see you struggling, I'll reach for your hand and help you back to shore.*

That night, as the waves lapped at our feet and the sun sank low, my hand slipped into Jake's. Not as two broken halves trying to complete each other, but as two whole souls, choosing to rise together.

My Return to Love

Once, in a workshop I was leading on the Itty Bitty Shitty Committee, we were exploring how it sabotages what we desire and how to move through those insecurities to return to love. Each of us wrote down the nastiest thing our inner critic says.

I'd taught this workshop countless times and expected the usual: *You're not good enough.* But that day, something darker clawed its way up. My hand shook as I wrote:

You messed up a good marriage to a good man who loved you.

You don't deserve love. You're unlovable.

You will be alone forever.

Time stopped. The words stared back like an old ghost. Even though I was back together with Jake, I could feel it—this wasn't the old "I'm not good enough." This was deeper. More tender. A layer I hadn't touched before. And there she was, Unlovable Ursula, still alive and kicking, echoing the pain of my failed marriage.

My Itty Bitty Shitty Committee pounced: *Really, Audrey? Crying in front of your students? Some teacher you are!*

The room blurred through my tears. My whole body wanted to run. Every instinct screamed: *Hide this. Stuff it down!* But then, beneath the roar, a whisper broke through:

The most beautiful people aren't perfect. They're the ones brave enough to be real.

So I took a breath. Named the voice. And chose to share it anyway. When it was my turn, my voice cracked as I said out loud, "You are unlovable. You will be alone."

And you know what happened? The women didn't run. They leaned in. Tears brimmed in their eyes too. Because the moment we drop our masks, we give others permission to do the same.

In that circle, I remembered a truth that lives in all of us: we are the same souls, with the same hidden fears and the same sacred desires to be loved, seen, and worthy.

This self-love journey is coming home to your whole self, again and again, instead of abandoning yourself. Each return reveals another layer, inviting you to know yourself more deeply and become more whole. Life will always offer opportunities to move through this spiral of remembrance.

After that workshop, I checked my phone and found a text from Jake: *Come home, I have good news.* When I walked in, candles flickered on the counter beside my favorite champagne. Jake beamed as he popped the cork.

"I got a job offer," he said. "In Seattle."

Seattle? The other side of the country. My smile faded. Inside, Ursula was screaming: *See? I told you. You're going to be alone. He's leaving!*

I braced myself for the breakup speech. Then Jake touched my shoulder, eyes steady and bright.

"Why are you crying? This is exciting!" He paused, then said, "I want you to move with me. I see myself marrying you. I want to build a life with you. I want to have little Audreys with you!"

The room spun. Not with fear this time, but gratitude. In that moment, I saw the truth:

Love didn't arrive because I fixed myself. It blossomed because I continue to embrace the parts I once exiled with compassion.

Jake was mirroring the love I was finally learning to give myself.

The real work isn't about erasing your shadows or trying to become someone else, but becoming more of who you *already* are...whole, free, authentically you. Letting every part of you—the messy, the tender, the wild—belong.

When you embrace your wholeness, your dark and your light, you don't just attract love.

You become it.

Not for someone else, but for yourself.

The Gift

The gift of befriending our shadows is liberation. Not just freedom from fear, but the freedom to be whole, authentic, sovereign, and fully expressed.

In Sanskrit, this liberation is called *moksha*, our truest purpose on this planet. Our purpose as humans isn't simply to grow or to feel good. It's to reclaim all of ourselves. To embody our most expansive self. To be free, whole, and wildly alive in our Truth. Not the ego's truth—but with a capital T—the Universal Truth that you are already whole, already enough, and you matter.

What if your soul chose *this* life, with every relationship, every shadow, and every trigger? Not as punishment, but as a portal guiding you back to your freedom and wholeness?

Compassion helps you remember what was never lost...your wholeness.

When you bring compassion to your shadows by listening, forgiving, and accepting, you dissolve judgment and clear the way for healing. Compassion doesn't fix you. It frees you. It gathers the fragments you once exiled and weaves them back into belonging.

This is the sacred reclamation and becoming the hero of your own story by meeting yourself with open hands and an open heart, and choosing love over shame.

This is liberation.

This is moksha.

This is the fierce, radiant freedom of being *fully you*.

And from this foundation of wholeness, you're ready for what comes next: meeting life's liminal spaces with curiosity, openness, and the courage to transform.

Integration

The Practice: Being With Your Triggers

Try this practice anytime you feel triggered by a shadow part. Then move through this breath practice:

1. Inhale: "I see you."

Name what's here: fear, jealousy, anger, failure. Naming creates space from the reactive mind and the triggered emotion. Space allows you conscious choice. You may recognize this shadow from your Wheel of Wholeness. You don't need to analyze it now, just be with it.

2. Exhale: "You belong."

Let your shoulders soften. Stay with the feeling instead of fighting it. Repeat this inhale–exhale until the charge begins to soften, even just a little.

3. Inhale: "What do you need?"

Listen gently. You may hear a whisper: rest, safety, honesty, a boundary, reassurance. Let the shadow tell you the truth it's been holding.

4. Closing

Place a hand on your heart and say:

"I choose compassion. I choose to accept all parts of me."

This is how you return to wholeness, one accepting breath at a time.

Reflection

- When I'm triggered, how does my shadow show up in my patterns, thoughts, and energy?
- What shadows feel hard to accept? The parts I hide, judge, or feel shame around?
- When I meet these parts with compassion, what truth or gift is revealed? What is the light on the other side of the shadow?

Vishuddha Chakra

Embracing Our Truest Expression

The fifth chakra, *Vishuddha*, sits at the base of your throat. It governs your expression, your boundaries, and the courage to share your truth. It's the bridge between your heart and your mind where compassion becomes clarity and your inner wisdom finds its way into words.

When this chakra is blocked, we swallow our needs, second-guess our intuition, or silence ourselves to stay small. You may feel it physically: a tight throat or neck, jaw tension, or that familiar lump when emotion rises but your voice doesn't.

But when this chakra is clear, your voice rises from wholeness, not fear. You speak from alignment and authenticity. You honor your boundaries without guilt. You express your truth without shrinking or shape-shifting. Your voice becomes your sovereignty made audible.

To balance this chakra, ask yourself:

- What part of me is hidden?
- What truth have I been swallowing, waiting to rise?

Each time you meet your shadows with compassion, you loosen the grip in your throat and free yourself to speak from your center instead of your fear. Your voice is not just sound. It's a vibration of your authenticity, the echo of your reclaimed truth.

Mantra

I AM WHOLE.
I AM ENOUGH.
I AM FREE.

CHAPTER 6

CURIOSITY

Trusting the Unknown and Opening to Magic

"Because you are alive, everything is possible."
−THICH NHAT HANH

Everyone has their "person." Mine is my dad. He's the reason I wrote this book. He always told me I was his greatest legacy. I hope this book becomes one of mine...for him, and for you. Whenever I was stuck in self-doubt, my dad reminded me of my power, saying, "You get to write your story."

It was October 22nd, 3:33 a.m., and I was restless. I was 36 weeks pregnant. My belly made sleep elusive, and my legs and back ached. Maybe it was the baby's way of preparing me for countless sleepless nights ahead. I reached for my cell phone and found a text from my mom that read: *Your dad passed away.*

Time stood still. I'm pretty sure my heart stopped beating too. No tears. No movement. I just froze in shock. The room, the air, my soul, all emptied at once. Silence roared. The night was black, unmoving. The only light came from the full moon.

I called my mom. She answered immediately, her voice cracking. After sitting on the couch for almost an hour, I inched down the long hallway back to our bedroom to wake up Jake. As soon as I stammered the words, "My dad is dead," everything in me unraveled. The dam behind my eyes and nose ruptured, flooding tears and snot.

Our cozy home is nestled on eight acres overlooking an undisturbed lake where small boats drift quietly fishing for trout. No one was around this early in the morning. Even the deer and our two eagle neighbors were fast asleep. It was as if Mother Earth herself held the land in a hush, in reverence for our sadness.

Jake and I silently shuffled to the car to drive to my parents' home. Giant Douglas fir trees loomed over us, and the moon peeked through the dark evergreen wall.

"Wow," breathed Jake, pointing to the sky. The moon was a colossal ball of bright orange and burnt sienna.

The moon has always had meaning for me, like it's looking down and guiding us, reminding us of life's rhythms. We cried and held each other in the quiet of the night, wrapped in the glow of that ancient light.

As we drove down the hill, the full moon followed us, perched above the freeway, lighting up the noir sky. I thought of my dad. Was he in that moonlight, escorting us to my mom's? I looked down at the clock. It was 5:55 a.m., a sign of angelic protection and life transition.

We whizzed up I-5 and picked up my mom in Everett, Washington, but by the time we turned around to return home, it was morning rush hour. Traffic would be a grueling two-hour bumper-to-bumper jam. A fitting start for the worst day of my life.

On our heavy ride home, I reflected on my bond with my dad. He was my best friend. We talked every day, sometimes multiple times a day. He listened to me unconditionally and patiently, for hours. You'd think at some point he would say, "Dude, can you ask me about my life?" But he never did. In the most giving and loving way, he was truly excited to help me live my fullest life and content to watch me grow. A selfless man, he also cared for my mom, thought of others, and always fought for people's rights. My eyes swelled. His life was cut too short.

Google Maps rerouted us away from the congested interstate traffic onto a quiet country road, and within minutes, onto another two-lane road. The sunrise peeked over the rolling farmland and vineyards, lifting me out of my fog. The darkness faded, and the sun skimmed the distant hills, lighting the sky in soft rose and lavender hues. A brief but potent moment of peace and awe, like Nature herself whispering in our grief, *Look over here. Don't fade. There's still beauty.*

I had never been on this road before and asked Jake, "Where are we? It's beautiful."

He shrugged, "Just following the GPS." He hadn't been on this road either.

My mom quietly whispered from the back seat, "This was your dad's favorite road to your house."

Magic.

This was my dad's gift right when we needed it most. Just like the moon had protected us through the darkness, he was now ushering us into the light. It felt like his way of saying: *Stay open, daughter. Even here, there is more to be seen.* When we loosen our controlling grip of how life should be and lean into life with curiosity, we discover our courage to meet the infinite and creative unknown with more trust and ease.

The Cost of Control

After my dad passed, I was dropped straight into one of those in-between spaces, the kind that shakes everything you thought you knew. I lost my favorite person, my rock, my biggest cheerleader, and my planned path.

Without his guidance, I felt helpless and alone. His death was that threshold for me—the ultimate liminal moment.

There's actually a word for these in-between seasons. The Latin word *limen* means "threshold" or "doorway." Liminal moments are transitions into the unknown: from what you know now into the uncharted future, from who you are today into who you're becoming.

Whether it's a move to a new city, a divorce, a new relationship, a death, a birth, a career change, going off to college, or retiring, these threshold moments stir up uncertainty and fear. They ask us to stand on the edge of what *was* and what *will be*, without a map for what comes next. Even though we may want to fast-forward through the discomfort, these moments become important initiations into who we're becoming.

Transitions can be so hard, because we're terrified that if we *really* let the unknown all the way in, it will break us. So the Itty Bitty Shitty Committee rushes in, gripping tighter, trying to outrun uncertainty or force things back into the familiar. Control keeps us busy, but it doesn't actually make us feel safe.

Maybe you know this feeling, gripping the steering wheel of life so tightly there's no room for anything new to unfold. You force the path, outline the timeline, and try to plan your way out of pain. The mind loops the past, rehearses the future, holding everything together so nothing falls apart.

Control feels protective, but it quietly suffocates our joy, our intuition, and the creative path that wants to move through us. And under the surface, it's always the same fear: *If I let go, will I still be safe?*

But the truth is, change is inevitable. We can't avoid it. What we can avoid is the chronic suffering we create by *resisting* the experience. Or as the Dalai Lama reminds us, "Pain is inevitable. Suffering is optional."

Suffering isn't the hard moment itself; it's the tightening around it. When we replay the story or fight the lesson, we stay stuck in the very pain we're trying to avoid. But when we meet the unknown from the softness of our hearts, through the open lens of curiosity, we create space to learn from it, and even to receive unexpected gifts.

I will never understand why my dad left this world too soon, and I can't say for certain that there is a reason for losing someone. But what I do know is that this moment transformed me into the person I was meant to be. I am a deeper, wiser, more empathetic person because of his life and death. Losing my dad forced me to find myself, my voice, and to become my own biggest supporter. It forced me to grow up and stop being so self-centered. Sorrow gave me the gift of a deeper reverence for life.

The path to transcend our pain is to lean into it. Only by entering the unknown, the places we fear most, can the unknown open us. And this is where **Curiosity** begins. When everything in you reaches for certainty, Curiosity becomes the handrail you hold when the ground beneath you gives way. It loosens the Itty Bitty Shitty Committee's grip and helps you stay with yourself as you walk into what you can't yet see. Curiosity doesn't demand certainty; it asks for presence. Curiosity doesn't erase the pain. It keeps you rooted in yourself long enough to let trust find you again.

Why Curiosity Matters

Curiosity was the gateway that helped me learn to trust myself again as I stepped into the unknown and became a mother without my father. And this is why curiosity matters for you, too. If you're in a season of change: heartbreak, grief, a diagnosis, a career shift, a new beginning, or simply feeling stuck, curiosity gives you the courage to meet the moment *as it is*, instead of bracing against it.

Let's get real, uncertainty is uncomfortable. When life shakes the ground beneath us, we scramble inside, dodging fear, numbing the ache, or clinging to what feels familiar, even when it no longer supports who we're becoming. Control feels safer than the unknown.

But the deeper question is this: how much of your energy is going into gripping what feels familiar simply because letting go feels terrifying?

The Itty Bitty Shitty Committee hates being caught off guard. So it tries to recreate the past, anticipate the future, and control the path, the timing, and the outcome. But it isn't the unknown that causes our suffering; it's the exhausting fight to *control* what was never ours to hold.

Here's why this matters: When we cling to the known, we drag yesterday into tomorrow and repeat the same patterns again and again. The "known" is really our past—our old wounds, old identities, old stories, and old habits. When we react from that place of the known, we can't move forward in the unknown. We stay stuck in the very loop we're trying to break.

When we insist we know, we can't grow.

When we insist we know, we can't grow. Only in the unknown is where infinite possibilities live.

And when we cling to control, our perspective narrows. We can't see the pathways, support, or creative solutions right in front of us. Because we're focused on controlling or avoiding the moment, we miss the signs, opportunities, and gentle nudges that could help us move forward with more ease. We only see one path—the one we're attached to—and overlook the many creative ways life is quietly opening.

Curiosity gets us unstuck. It becomes the bridge. From fear to possibility, from gripping to allowing, from control to trust. It softens our hold. It widens our view. It helps us stay open long enough to receive what this moment is trying to show us. Curiosity expands our perspective so we can finally *see* something new and *do* something new.

Curiosity helps us take the courageous step forward and trust again. To trust in life, trust in the timing, and trust in ourselves. It's where the fight ends and the softening begins. And that's where freedom lives: not in forcing the moment, but in meeting it with presence, a new lens, and an open heart.

Self-Love Tool #4: Curiosity

Curiosity is the practice of expanding your perspective and meeting the moment with fresh eyes, allowing something new to reveal itself.

By now, you've experienced the power of the first three C's: **Consciousness** wakes you back into presence, **Care** tends to the younger you within, and **Compassion** integrates the parts you once pushed away. **Curiosity** is the practice of staying open long enough for the next step to reveal itself.

Curiosity isn't about fixing or figuring anything out. It's the opposite. It's letting the moment be what it is and choosing to meet it with openness instead of resistance. When we meet the unknown with curiosity, fear can shift into faith, problems into possibilities, and contraction into expansion.

Curiosity shows us how to loosen our grip and see the challenge with a new perspective. It invites gentler questions, more openness, and the willingness to notice what we once missed. It helps us stay open to the signs, whispers, and invitations we might have overlooked when we were contracting in fear.

Just like a child, curiosity invites wonder and imagination: asking questions without needing answers, exploring without a fixed destination, and taking the next courageous step even if we can't yet see where it leads.

Curiosity brings us back to the present moment. It's only in the present moment that a new future begins. This is where curiosity walks beside you, helping you meet the unknown with steadiness and faith.

Curiosity opens what control contracts.

Curiosity changes our perspective. And when we change how we perceive an experience, we change how we experience it. Curiosity opens what control contracts. Through it, we begin to trust that what is meant for us will stay, and what is not will gently fall away. We flow with life, instead of resisting it.

Now, let's explore how to practice it.

The Curiosity Reset

When we feel overwhelmed, afraid, ungrounded, or gripping for control, the Itty Bitty Shitty Committee spins into the "what ifs," the imagined futures, and the looping pasts that pull us out of the present. Curiosity can't live in the "what ifs." It can only live here, *now*, in this moment. Presence is where you reclaim your clarity and your inner knowing. When you return to the now, you make space for truth to arise from within.

Practicing curiosity helps us meet life with more ease, especially when things don't go according to plan. When life "lifes" hard, the Itty Bitty Shitty Committee kicks into overdrive. It tries to control the narrative, the outcome, and the timeline. But gripping harder only creates more tension. Underneath it all, we're resisting what *is*. And that *resistance* is what keeps us stuck.

Trying to stay in control often looks like gripping a relationship that ended, clinging to a plan you thought your life would follow, or expecting life to unfold exactly as you imagined.

So how do we loosen that grip? Here's a simple reset to practice curiosity in the exact moments you feel yourself bracing against life.

Step 1: Pause The Story

When you feel yourself caught in control or resistance, first ask: *Whose business am I in?* As author and teacher, Byron Katie teaches, "There are only three kinds of business: mine, yours, and God's." Too often we slip into other people's business—our expectations of them, their choices, their reactions—or into God's business, trying to control life's timing and outcomes. The moment we do, we lose our peace.

This question widens your perspective and helps you meet the moment without forcing it to be something else. It loosens the grip of "how it should be" and gently returns you to the truth of what *is*.

When you let go of what you can't control, you make space for what you can: your energy, your presence, your peace. This question stops the Itty Bitty Shitty Committee's story and brings you back to the only place curiosity can live: *your own business*, right here. Your thoughts. Your actions. This moment.

Step 2: Come Back To Your Body

Next, reconnect with your body so you can soften into the moment instead of bracing against it.

Place one hand on your heart and one on your belly to remind you: *I'm here.*

Inhale, inviting calm, trust, and ease.

Exhale gently, releasing what isn't yours to carry.

Just as the waves carry sand from the shore and return it again, let your breath remind you: There is no shortage. There is only ebb and flow.

When my dad died, I disappeared into shock and fear, then I placed my hand on my heart and remembered to breathe. That touch anchored me back into the only place I had any ground, right here. It's a forever practice of coming back to the moment, to meet yourself, as you are. The same is true for you. When you arrive in your body, you come home to yourself again.

Curiosity begins with this homecoming of remembering: *I am here. I am safe. I am held.*

Step 3: Open To Wonder & Possibility

As you practice softening your control, Curiosity begins to shift how you meet life's challenges, detours, and unknowns. Your perspective widens. You begin to meet life the way a child does...open, soft, and willing to greet what's here with wonder instead of fear.

When we get curious about what we're resisting and why, something inside begins to loosen. Possibility replaces panic. Softness replaces the scramble. The moment opens. And in that opening, even the most familiar experience can reveal something new.

From this gentler place, you might try asking one simple curios question:

What else could be true here?

Or

What is this moment here to teach me?

Curiosity teaches us to live the question instead of gripping for the answer.

As adults, we often lose the spark of wonder, falling into routines, repeating old thoughts, and carrying yesterday into today. Curiosity doesn't demand the whole path. It simply invites one shift in how you see, one softening in your heart, one courageous step. Through curiosity, even the ordinary becomes extraordinary.

Each time you return to your own business, release the grip of control, and ask a more generous question, you create a new future, one calm, curious moment at a time.

Life is complex and unpredictable. But when we feel adrift, being present and curious is our raft home steadying us, softening us, and leading us gently forward. And sometimes curiosity doesn't move us forward at all. It simply invites us to pause, to rest, and to trust the quiet seasons where nothing seems like it's happening.

Wintering

When we're in a season of deep transition, stepping into the unknown can feel grueling and scary. It's like winter—quiet, stark, and stripped down. Winter can look still or barren on the surface, but beneath that stillness, life is already at work. Roots are being tended to, what no longer serves is composting, and seeds are germinating.

If you're moving through a season of winter, it's a calling to hibernate and go inward, to rest, reflect, and remember. Healing can't be forced or rushed. If we try to control it, the lessons return until they're fully integrated.

There is no shortcut to Spring. Healing happens on its own time. Our work is to allow our feelings to be heard and trust that we are unfolding perfectly. Winter isn't failure; it's part of the preparation. It's where the roots grow.

Let everything you thought "should be" wither, freeze, and compost. Winter is where old identities dissolve and new life quietly begins to form beneath the surface. When you allow yourself to rest into the healing powers of repose, reflection, curiosity, and self-study, while staying present and awake to life's whispers, you remember you are exactly where you're supposed to be. Often, in the darkness, you're at the beginning of something new.

Think back to a winter in your life, a time you felt stuck or afraid. You couldn't see it then, but something essential was germinating beneath the surface. In the quiet, what isn't true begins to fall away. False beliefs, outdated identities, old habits that no longer resonate with who you are becoming. Often we must descend into the dark for that wisdom to be revealed. And from that stillness something truer begins to emerge. And you did emerge stronger, wiser, more rooted in yourself, proof that winter was shaping you in ways you couldn't yet name.

Often, our fear of the unknown is far greater than any hardship we actually endure. The Itty Bitty Shitty Committee will try to convince you that uncertainty is dangerous, but winter is simply the part of the cycle where you can't yet see the bloom. The paradox of curiosity is that it asks us to stay open to possibilities, yet also reminds us that there is only one true way forward: the way that comes from the heart and expresses its truth.

Only in the present moment can you touch this inner knowing. That's why winter invites quiet. Stillness. Deep listening. It's no accident that the words *silent* and *listen* share the same letters. When the mind softens and the noise settles, you can finally hear what's been trying to reach you all along—your truth, your forgotten dreams, and the wisdom of the heart. Curiosity keeps your heart open long enough to hear what life is trying to show you.

The more you soften into stillness, the more you'll trust yourself and the quiet timing of your own unfolding.

So, immerse yourself in the solitude of winter. Breathe in the season's wisdom. Be with your fears, your pain, your triumphs, and most importantly, be with yourself. Trust the quiet alchemy of this season. You'll discover the unknown was never empty; it was preparing you all along. And you'll see that the newness of each moment is a wellspring of creativity and wisdom.

> *Curiosity keeps us open long enough to witness what is quietly being born.*

Just like winter softens us for spring, curiosity softens our grip on control and makes room for life to bloom in ways we couldn't plan. It's not about rushing through the hard seasons, but learning to walk with them with presence, with trust, with wonder.

Curiosity is what helps us move from the waiting room of the unknown into the next chapter of our lives. Curiosity keeps us open long enough to witness what is quietly being born.

Birth

After a long winter season, there are moments when life cracks you open reminding you that even in the deepest darkness, something new has already been stirring.

The day my dad died was slow. I gazed out the window, hoping he would walk across the lawn and cheerily ask everyone, "Why the long faces?" Later, I wandered to the edge of the lake, my tears blurring everything around me. When I finally looked up, I noticed dozens of dragonflies circling around me, as if this spirit animal was reminding me of magic, the other realm, and life's beauty, even in the midst of heartbreak.

As the saffron moon began to rise over the still lake, the black water rippling in sweet zigzags beneath it, my mind went back to a conversation my dad and I had on names for my future daughter. He was so excited I was having a girl. Jake and I were torn between two names. Dad loved one of them: *Hunter*. He said it was a "powerful, badass name, a force to be reckoned with."

My tear-soaked eyes turned the luminous moon into a glossy blob. I exhaled, "I miss you, Dad." The ache felt unbearable, and the moon grew bigger and brighter, as if he were answering, *I'm still with you. I'm watching you. I'm protecting you.*

Later that evening, I looked at my phone and the first news story that appeared read: *Tonight's annual orange moon is called the Hunter's Moon.*

More magic.

Almost two weeks later, we viewed my dad's body at the funeral home. His face looked peaceful, almost as if he were only sleeping. His hands were gently folded over his heart. I touched them and cried all over him. Grief hollowed me in a way I hadn't known was possible.

The next day, Jake took photos of me and the henna tattoo my artist friend had painted on my pregnant belly in remembrance of my dad. It was a drawing of the Hunter's Moon and dragonflies. The word "Allow" was painted on my forearm, reminding me to surrender to life's flow.

That afternoon, my water broke.

We laid my father down on Friday, and the very next day, our baby girl, Hunter, was born. As my dad had predicted, she came into the world with a powerful and radiant force, living up to her name. Hunter and my dad missed each other by thirteen days, but they are infinitely linked in love.

I truly believe he placed her in our arms early as an unexpected mercy, a pause on my heartbreak.

Even now, I carry both sorrow and love in my heart. Curiosity helped me soften around the edges of my pain, loosen my grip on how life "should" have been, and open me to the beauty and mystery of what was unfolding.

Meeting myself in uncertainty, I've also let myself be okay with not being okay. I can be with the anger and injustice I feel about my dad's death, and also trust what is not mine to control.

Practicing Curiosity allowed me to feel my feelings while opening to deeper joy and appreciation for the love my dad gave and the legacy he left. We are vast beings with the capacity to feel deeply. Curiosity helps us be bigger than our past without leaving it behind.

Having experienced the worst loss of my life and given birth to one of the greatest joys of my life, I've learned how life and death are intertwined. Both are inevitable, unpredictable, raw, and honest. They wake us up to the gift of presence and to life's impermanence, fragility, magnificence, and simple beauties.

Oddly, death taught me how to live.

After death, new life was born. My daughter and a deeper, wiser me.

If we're blessed to be on this earth long enough, we will experience loss: a death, a diagnosis, a trauma, a miscarriage, a divorce, a heartbreak, a shedding of an outdated identity. But coming out the other side, we can gain a deeper reverence for life.

If we want a rich and meaningful life, we've got to be here for *all* of it. Curiosity reminds us to surrender to what is, let go of control, and trust that even in seasons of loss, life is still quietly shaping something new. And in time, what once felt unbearable can soften into something new.

The Gift

The gift of curiosity is trust in ourselves and in the unfolding of a greater Universe that supports us in ways our minds could never plan. Curiosity relaxes our grip on certainty and opens us to the quiet wisdom of uncertainty, offering us freedom from old conditioning and the wisdom and faith to create anew.

Life is never static or predictable. When we cling to control, we step out of life's natural rhythm. When we open to curiosity, we step back into it. Curiosity about the unknown helps us stay present and trust life's creative movement.

Curiosity invites us to move with life's harmonious dance and to remember that we, too, are an essential part of Life's sacred rhythm.

Mother Earth shows us this truth. She never rushes, and yet she's always on time, trusting each moment to unfold in its own perfect timing. She moves in cycles, in seasons, in sacred rhythms of birth, death, and renewal. Trees surrender their leaves to winter to make space for spring. Night morphs into day. You and I were born in the creative darkness of our mothers' wombs. We are part of these same cycles, held by the same rhythm of life where everything transforms in its own time.

> *Curiosity invites us to move with life's harmonious dance and to remember that we, too, are an essential part of Life's sacred rhythm.*

And though the unknown can feel dark, that darkness is not empty or dangerous. It is fertile. It is where roots deepen, where unseen transformation begins. When we embrace it with curiosity, we meet life in all its mystery, complexity, wonder, pain, and glory.

Curiosity is what carries us across the liminal spaces, the quiet bridge between what was and what will be, so we can meet the next chapter of our lives with trust instead of fear.

Curiosity helps us navigate life's impermanence, rooting us in the ever-new present. It rekindles creativity, imagination, and possibility. Each time we practice curiosity, we peel back another layer of fear. Saying yes to our present experience opens us to the quiet miracles within and around us. What once felt fixed begins to loosen. What once felt impossible begins to breathe.

Curiosity stretches time and enriches our experience. It awakens our wonder, like children seeing the miraculous in the mundane again. Although this moment may look like one that's come before, it's not, and it never will be again. Each moment arrives with its own truth and intricacy.

So be here. Soften here. Let curiosity widen your heart. Practicing curiosity helps you trust that life is happening *through* you and *for* you, in its own divine timing.

Trust that you are unfolding beautifully, like the seasons, like the tides, like the endless rhythm of life itself. Curiosity returns you to that rhythm, the one beneath your fear, beneath your stories, beneath the noise to the quiet pulse that has been carrying you all along.

Integration

The Practice: Devotional Daydreaming

Devotional daydreaming is a gentle practice of releasing control and opening yourself to possibility. It's not about forcing clarity or figuring things out. It's about creating space for wisdom to arrive on its own time.

Have you ever noticed how the answers you're searching for rarely come when you're forcing them? The name on the tip of your tongue. The creative solution you can't quite access. They often arrive on a walk, in the shower, or in the quiet hours of the night when the mind stops trying so hard.

When we stop forcing answers, the nervous system settles. The mind relaxes its grip, and creativity begins to flow again. This is often when truth rises, not from effort, but from ease. Devotional daydreaming invites that same openness, but with intention.

How to Practice:

- Set aside one to five minutes each day.
- Relax your body. Place a hand on your heart or belly and deepen your breath.
- Let your mind wander...not aimlessly, but with devotion to your truest, freest self. Devotion to the deep desires in your heart and what matters most.
- Instead of asking *What should I do?*, ask: *How do I want to feel?*
- Let images, sensations, or feelings arise without analyzing them.
- No action required. The key here is to not need an answer or figure out a solution. Let the mind wander with wonder instead of analyzing and calculating.

You might practice this while standing by water, walking among trees, or sitting quietly without your phone to remind you of Nature's rhythm.

This is curiosity in its most receptive form. A practice of trusting that when we stop forcing clarity, something deeper begins to speak.

For now, let yourself dream. Let yourself feel. Let yourself ask questions without needing the answers. Let the seeds take their time. This is a practice of opening to Curiosity by letting go of control and receiving more creativity.

Reflection

- Where in your life are you *gripping* for control instead of *allowing*?
- What else could be true in the situation you're facing right now?
- What is this moment inviting you to notice?

Ajna Chakra

Trusting The Unseen

The sixth chakra, the *Ajna* chakra, is your third eye, located between your eyebrows. Its name means "to know." It's the center of intuition and inner vision. Represented by indigo light, it helps you sense truth beyond logic, guiding you toward what is becoming, not just what has been.

Your two physical eyes see the world as it appears. Your Ajna sees the unseen, the gentle shimmer of possibility.

To bring this chakra into harmony, practice leaning into the unknown with curiosity rather than fear. Curiosity softens the mind's grip on certainty and opens you to intuition, the quiet wisdom that has always been guiding you.

Close your eyes and bring your awareness to the space between your brows.

Ask yourself:

- What truth is quietly rising beneath the noise?
- What is my intuition wanting me to know right now?

Notice where in your body feel restrictive and where it feels open. Pay attention to the subtle nudges, synchronicities, and inner whispers that follow. Like the moon and the seasons, your intuition moves in rhythms. Curiosity helps you listen to those rhythms and trust their timing.

You are guided. You are held. Your inner sight always knows the way home.

Mantra

I AM OPEN AND TRUST THE INFINITE POSSIBILITIES THAT AWAIT ME AND ARE WITHIN ME.

CHAPTER 7

CONNECTION

Aligning with Your Truest, Sovereign Self

*"You are not a drop in the ocean, you are the
entire ocean in a drop."*

—RUMI

Life has a rhythm. Magic, mystery, and sacred unfolding reveal themselves when we slow down enough to notice. But back in 2021, I couldn't see any of it.

It was Christmas 2021. The tree lights twinkled in the corner, wrapping paper scattered across the floor, but the room felt heavy. I sat on the couch, weighed down by exhaustion, shame, and resentment, wondering where the vibrant, carefree woman I had been before motherhood had gone.

The year had been good in many ways and also overly full. Buying and remodeling a new home, welcoming another baby at age 42, while raising a highly emotional toddler. Despite many dreams coming true, my in-person teaching business had vanished overnight because of the COVID pandemic, taking with it my sense of purpose. I felt ashamed of my ungratefulness, but the truth was undeniable—I was drifting further from myself.

The daily realities felt like too much for my nervous system to hold. My three-month-old was limp and quiet, pooping every ten days, needing weekly physical therapy. My toddler wasn't sleeping, melting down daily, peeing on the floor. One afternoon I was breastfeeding my baby while my toddler stood across the hall, red-faced, screaming and glaring at me with so much rage in her eyes. I was crying too, tears soaking my shirt, chest tight, body trembling. In that moment, I thought: *This is not the mother I want to be.* I was unraveling, anxious, scattered, and disconnected from my spark, pouring into everyone with nothing left for myself.

On Christmas morning, I unwrapped a gift from Jake, a handmade coupon book titled "Believe in You 2022." Inside were little lifelines: brunch with friends, a massage, an online spiritual retreat. It was such a thoughtful gift, but it pierced me with the hard truth that my struggles were visible to everyone around me.

I wish I could say that from there, my postpartum anxiety lifted and everything clicked back into place. But growth doesn't happen like that. Healing is rarely neat or linear. It's messy, cyclical, and asks us to sit with discomfort longer than we'd like. Back then, survival was the only rhythm I knew.

My Itty Bitty Shitty Committee compared me to other moms who seemed to have it all together—crafting with their kids, baking homemade sourdough, posting selfies in their perfectly styled top knots—while I was lucky if I managed a shower. I felt like I was drowning.

So I started small. Pathetically small. Locking myself in the bathroom, breathing long and slow while my toddler whined outside the door and I cried back, "Mommy's going potty!" Those two minutes became sacred. They were mine alone. Slowly, those bathroom breaks stretched into five minutes of meditation in the morning. Then journaling. Little by little, I started to return to stillness, to write, to breathe, to hear the tiniest whispers of my own spirit again.

The 5 C's I share in this book helped me learn to mother myself and find my spark again. My inner child needed tenderness, my shadows needed compassion, my heart needed more spaciousness of curiosity instead of forcing and control. And perhaps most of all, I needed to reconnect to my spirit again.

What felt like a dark hole I was trying to claw out of slowly began to shift into something else. Life was inviting me to stop resisting the season I was in and lean into motherhood, not as an *interruption* of my path, but as an *initiation* into a deeper becoming.

Healing was slow and messy. My harsh expectations of who I "should" be kept me anxious and resentful. But the more I accepted the season I was in, the less I struggled with my present experience. The practice of connecting with my soul and nurturing my spirit offered me more patience, presence, and a flicker of hope.

And here's the truth: I haven't "arrived." I am still aligning, still practicing, still remembering my worth and working on connecting to my truest self *every. single. day.*

It's not through more *pushing* or *perfecting*, but through *purification* that we connect more deeply to our truest self. This is a lifetime journey—for me, for you, for all of us—to shed the false layers of the Itty Bitty Shitty Committee and return again and again to our most authentic and free selves, where our truest self can lead. Each time we return, we come back with more depth and a new way of seeing. This is the sacred spiral of life, always inviting us to know ourselves deeply and live more truly.

Life has a natural rhythm, and you are an essential part of it.

We'll all get pulled out of alignment by fear or life's challenges, and still, connection to our true self always shows us the way back home.

Those two and a half years of finding my way back to myself felt like a dark tunnel. But that tunnel was not an end. It was a chamber of transformation. The self I thought I had to be was dissolving so that my truer self could emerge. These cocoon seasons are uncomfortable, sometimes painfully so, but they are necessary. We release what no longer resonates with who we are meant to be, letting old identities die and surrender to the evolution. In that darkness, we're not stuck. We're becoming. Eventually, we're ready to rise.

If you've been feeling lost, broken, or stuck, maybe you're in your own cocoon of transformation right now. It might feel dark and cramped. It might feel like everything is falling apart. But trust that you are in the middle of something much bigger. You are evolving in ways you can't yet see.

Life has a natural rhythm, and you are an essential part of it. By quieting the Itty Bitty Shitty Committee, we remember who we really are, a reflection of the Divine. When we connect with our true selves and remember who we already are—expansive, ever-creative, infinite—fear loses its grip.

Connection isn't just about relationships with others. It's about alignment with your soul, your truest self. And when you begin to find that alignment again, everything changes.

Self-Love Tool #5: Connection

The number one way we abandon ourselves is by getting lost in the Itty Bitty Shitty Committee's stories of judgment, lack, fear, and "shoulds." These stories siphon our power and pull us into a vortex of doubt. When we listen to the Committee's demands, we forget what our heart already knows: who we truly are.

Connection is how you come home again. It's alignment with your Soul, your truest and freest self. When you're aligned, you don't have to be anything other than who you are. You don't have to do more or prove your worth. Worthiness is your birthright, not something you chase, but something you remember. The Divine created you with your exact story, gifts, and voice. You were chosen for this moment, on this planet. Your work is simply to become who you already are.

When you lose connection with this truth, life feels uphill. You overthink, you doubt yourself, you chase worth outside of you. But when you reconnect, your breath deepens, your shoulders soften, time stretches. You feel grounded, present, and guided. You begin to feel the sacred hum of life moving *with* you instead of *against* you. Synchronicities show up. Joy flickers through ordinary moments. You remember: you are not lost. You are led.

The Divine has planted unique gifts and longings within you, quiet seeds meant to be tended over time. When you nurture them, you're gently guided toward your *dharma*, your soul's purpose.

In Sanskrit, *yoga* means "to yoke" or "to unite." And this is what connection truly is: the union of your human self with the infinite soul you came here to embody.

Connection is the self-love tool that helps you embrace all of who you innately are so you can create what only you can bring into the world. When you are united with your most authentic self, your path reveals itself. Your dharma isn't something you hunt for. It's something you allow, through alignment, through ease, through living in a way that feels like truth.

Dharma: Your Soul's Calling

Your *dharma*, your soul's purpose, is why you're here. It isn't just a job title or a role. It's the way your soul moves through whatever you do, the *why* beneath the *what*.

Living in alignment with your soul's purpose connects you to the invisible thread that links you back to Source, to creativity, weaving you with the infinite possibility of your destiny. Spiritual teacher Sahara Rose says, "Your dharma...is the unique vibration that your soul carries to everything that you do and every way that you are."

While the mind *pushes* you to do more for the sake of your false self, dharma gently *pulls* you toward healing, growth, and authentic expression. The ego pushes, but your dharma pulls. One feels like grasping, the other like flowing. When you're connected to your higher self and let the heart lead, life leaves you breadcrumbs, small luminous signs that you're on your path. And if you're questioning your path, that questioning is often the call.

Does life always feel easeful? Of course not. But when you align with your true self, you begin to notice the difference between the inner critic's noise and your soul's quiet yes. There's a subtle shift inside you...a softening, a remembering. Sometimes it's a body cue, a breath that drops you back into yourself, your intuition that knows, a heart that stirs. You've felt these moments before, the ones that feel like truth even when you can't explain why. That's your dharma calling.

Your dharma is always whispering, inviting you into your fullest expression, into the unfolding of your soul's blueprint already written within you. Every breadcrumb, every nudge, every synchronicity is life guiding you home to your truest self. When we honor this blueprint, we live a life of deeper meaning and real fulfillment.

Dharma doesn't give you worth. It reveals the worth that's been there all along. And when you follow that call and connect to your true self, you begin to feel it in your body: a lightness, an ease, a quiet knowing. It's that mysterious moment where you and life move as one, where the path unfolds and the rhythm of life carries you. This is flow, the experience of connection in motion.

Flow: The Experience of Connection in Motion

Flow isn't something you chase. It's what naturally rises when you're in alignment with your true self. When you're connected, you don't have to force life. You remember you're part of life's rhythm, and that rhythm carries you. Flow feels like ease. Not because life is easy, but because you're no longer fighting it or yourself.

The late psychologist Mihaly Csikszentmihalyi described "flow" as a state where you're so fully absorbed in what you're doing that the experience becomes its own reward. Psychologists call it "flow," artists call it "the groove," athletes call it "the zone." I call it Connection, a moment so alive that time bends, the mind quiets, and the heart leads. Flow is what happens when your soul leads and fear steps aside.

My husband, Jake, an adventure enthusiast, describes flow as "Type 2 Fun," like scaling a steep mountain where he might even die (but doesn't), because he's so focused and present. He becomes one with the mountain, joyfully absorbed in the climb. That's his way of finding connection. *I would pee in my pantalones!* But that's the beauty. Connection shows up differently for all of us. His is on a mountaintop. Yours might be in the kitchen cooking, on the yoga mat, deep in a soulful conversation, or creating something new. The key is knowing yourself and nurturing your spirit so you can recognize the signs of your own alignment.

And flow doesn't only show up inside you. It shows up around you. Life mirrors your alignment back to you through synchronicities, those tiny winks from the universe that whisper, "You're on the right path." You think of a friend and they text. You've been longing for guidance and the exact podcast or book appears. You've been hoping for an opportunity and someone introduces you to the right person at the perfect time. These magical alignments aren't random. They're confirmations of connection, reminders that when you're in authentic alignment, life meets you.

Flow isn't just about action. It's a state of being, a way of feeling. We are human *beings*, after all, not human *doings*. In true connection, the boundary between doing and being dissolves. The artist becomes the paintbrush, the story writes itself, the dancer is danced. The Divine moves through us when we are connected to our true selves, when doing and being become one, and inspired effort meets effortless ease.

Connection doesn't mean perfection or permanent bliss. It isn't constant happiness. It's remembering you're part of a bigger rhythm, and your soul already knows the steps. Flow begins the moment you stop trying to be who you think you "should" be and allow yourself to be who you already are. Alignment is your birthright. The natural state of a soul co-creating with God, Source, the Divine.

The vibrancy of this state is fragile. Life will pull us out through distractions, challenges, and the noise of the Itty Bitty Shitty Committee. It's normal to fall out of flow. It's human. Through **intention, attention, embodiment,** and **surrender** we return, again and again, to the current of our own soul.

Intention

The Upanishads, ancient Vedic texts from India, teach, "You are what your deepest desire is." When an intention is rooted in the heart, it connects you to your soul's purpose, who you are here to be, and how you are meant to feel.

Intention is both the *blueprint* and the *compass* for our dreams. It's the *big vision* of what we want and the *roadmap* for living this vision in each moment. There is our *soul's intention,* the deeper desire of who we are meant to be; and our *daily intention,* the energy we want to embody today. Both are found the same way: by tuning into the quiet truth of your heart.

When we move with our true intention, we stop reacting to life and begin to flow with it.

Ask your heart:

- What is my deepest desire?
- Who am I meant to be?

- How do I want to feel today, and what one small choice would honor that?

Let your breath settle. Let your Soul whisper its quiet wisdom.

Living with intention is not about manifesting an outcome. Manifestation is a by-product of being in alignment with your truest self. When your intention comes from fear, it drains you. When it comes from the heart, it roots you.

And once your heart sets the compass, your attention is what carries you forward.

Attention

If intention is the *why* and the *what*, then attention is the *how*. Attention is the actions and beliefs that bring your intention to life. It's where you place your energy and focus.

You're always giving your attention to something. The question is, to what?

When your attention is led by the Itty Bitty Shitty Committee, it sabotages your potential. But when your attention flows from your soul, it serves your intention of who you want to be and what you are here to create. Attention driven by the mind contracts; attention guided by the heart expands.

Is my attention right now serving my dreams or sabotaging them?

So why does this matter? Attention gives your intention momentum. Without attention, your intention stays a wish. With attention, your focus becomes your dream in motion.

Ask yourself:

- Is my attention right now serving my dreams or sabotaging them?
- Where do I need to place my attention to be my fullest expression?

Attention is how you line your moment-to-moment choices up with your soul's intention.

And this is where embodiment comes in, when attention shifts from something you *do* into something you naturally *are*.

Embodiment

Embodiment is where attention becomes lived. It's the moment alignment stops being a concept and becomes something you feel— subtle, steady, and real. When Connection is embodied, it moves from thought into felt truth: joy, harmony, and an ease that already lives within you.

Embodiment is remembering who you are and practicing it in real time. Embodiment is the shift from *efforting* to *allowing*, from *striving* to *becoming*. You return to your true self through devotion, not discipline.

Embodiment is how you connect to your spirit and nurture your inner flame, listening for what she needs, honoring it, and letting your life reflect that truth. Three doorways into this daily devotion are **getting quiet, giving,** and **gratitude.**

Getting quiet opens the channel to your inner wisdom. The Itty Bitty Shitty Committee thrives on noise, distractions, and chaos. When you quiet the mind, you open to the Divine.

You receive guidance from your heart and soul: truth, creativity, love, and peace. The answers you seek are waiting in the quiet space of your heart's wisdom. The mind shouts, but the heart whispers. Embodiment begins when you learn to hear it, and follow it.

Try this daily ritual: place one hand on your heart and the other on your womb space (or your proverbial womb) within you that creates, feels, and knows. Take five slow breaths and gently ask, *What message do you have for me?* Then listen.

As you listen, you begin to tend a relationship with your inner wisdom, your spirit.

Honor whatever arises. These whispers know the way. As you build a relationship with your intuitive spirit, it will guide you toward what you need. It may be stepping outside for a moment of sun, walking barefoot in the grass, slowing down to be more present, loosening your grip on what the mind is clenching, or release what's been held through sound or movement. Follow these invitations. They are how alignment finds you again.

Just a few sacred minutes builds trust with your inner knowing. Think of it as a devotion to your inner world: a daily remembering, a returning, a soft place to come home.

Giving expands your spirit. The inner critic hoards, but your soul expands. Giving what you most desire helps you rise above the Alignment Line immediately. If you long for love, give love. If you want abundance, be generous. Even small acts, a kind word, a smile, a thoughtful gesture lift your vibration and remind you of your true nature. Giving redirects you from the ego's self-importance into service, connection, and your true self.

And giving isn't just outward. It's also to yourself. Get to know your own spirit and the qualities that make you *you*.

Ask your heart: *What does my spirit need to feel nurtured today?* Is it rest, play, creativity? Then honor that. This is how you tend your spark.

Gratitude shifts your frequency. It's one of the simplest, most powerful ways to elevate your energy. When the Itty Bitty Shitty Committee drags you into problems, gratitude clears the fog so you can see the beauty and magic already here. Even on the hardest days when you're heartbroken, strapped for cash, or in conflict, gratitude softens the edges. I've noticed in my own marriage that when I shift from blame to appreciation, even silently in my own heart, the energy between us changes.

Try this: each evening, name three moments, ordinary or extraordinary, that you're grateful for. The more you notice, the more you realize what a gift it is to be alive.

Getting quiet, giving, and **gratitude** are three doorways into embodied connection. They return you to the spark within you and the spark of Life. From that place of alignment with your true self, synchronicities appear, joy rises, and you remember: you are already on the path your soul is longing to walk.

Connection deepens as we move from intention to attention to embodiment, but there is always one final invitation: surrender.

Surrender: Letting Go To Let In

Surrender is the open hand that allows flow and makes space for grace. It isn't something you force; it's something you allow. Manifestation isn't created by pushing; it's a byproduct of alignment. When you align with your true self, life reflects that frequency back to you. Manifestation is simply alignment made visible.

Alignment asks us to trust the mystery.

In the 1989 film *Indiana Jones and the Last Crusade,* Indy stands at the edge of a vast cavern in search of the Holy Grail. The chasm is impossibly wide, the drop beneath him invisible and endless. There is no bridge, no rope, no way across.

Only when we trust enough to move in alignment does the ground appear beneath us. That's surrender.

He knows the final step of the journey requires a leap of faith. So he closes his eyes, gathers his courage, and steps forward into what looks like the void.

And then something remarkable happens. The invisible bridge appears beneath his feet to support him.

In life, we often have to take the intentional step before we see the path. Only when we trust enough to move in alignment does the ground appear beneath us. That's surrender.

Surrender isn't apathy; it's courage. It's releasing attachment to the outcome, not from laziness but from trust. When your *attention* aligns with your *intention*, action begins to arise from your true self.

Letting go of the outcome and of our agenda is so hard, but it's essential. When we release control over *how* our path must play out, we free ourselves from rigidity and open to possibilities we never could have scripted. When we accept where we are and release how things "should" be, we step into the present moment where our power lives.

Surrender isn't doing nothing. It's taking aligned action while releasing the demand that life unfolds in the exact way or timeline your mind imagined.

When we hold too tightly, we choke the possibilities life is trying to bring us. Pressure narrows the pathways for creativity. Trust opens them. White-knuckling blocks the dream; loosening your grip lets something even better through.

Think of the thing you once believed you had to have—the job, the relationship, the accomplishment—only to realize later the closed door was protection or redirection. Surrender reveals what forcing never can: ease, alignment, and often something better than you imagined.

What is meant for you will find you. And what isn't meant for you will slowly fall away no matter how tightly you try to hold it. Surrender is trusting that life is not withholding from you, but guiding you.

So how do we practice surrender?

It begins with a simple shift: loosening our grip on the outcome and returning to the present moment. When we stop forcing the path and instead align our attention, intention, and action with our truest self, surrender becomes less about giving up control and more about trusting the unfolding. Here's a simple way to begin.

Try a Surrender Ritual:

Write down what you're gripping too tightly: a dream, a relationship, a resentment, an old story, an expectation or timeline. Safely burn the paper or bury it in the earth, offering it back to Source.

As you release it, whisper three times: "I trust the path and am open to something even better."

Surrender isn't about giving up. It's about lightening up. It's releasing the weight of the past and the pressure of controlling the future so you can meet this moment. Open, trusting, alive. When your actions arise from a light heart, you are already co-creating with the Divine. The outcome comes in its right timing.

Sparkle: Signs of Alignment

When we surrender, the signs arrive as tiny sparkles, small reminders and synchronicities that Divine connection is everywhere. You are being guided, always inviting you to align with your truest self and become one with Divine Source.

It was Thanksgiving, and my daughter, Hunter, had just turned five. Instead of making a turkey, Jake, the kids, his parents, my mom, and I piled into the minivan and drove to see the snow. As the car climbed toward Mount Rainier, my mind wandered back to Bali six months earlier, where I had carried some of my dad's ashes to release into the Indian Ocean.

I had dreamed of the perfect moment, his ashes carried gently into the horizon, waves closing with ceremony. But instead, his ashes clung to my toes, my little offering of bamboo leaves and flowers washing stubbornly back to shore. I stood there in tears, wondering if I had ruined it.

Then, in that quiet way only he could, I heard my dad's voice: *Try again at the waterfall in Ubud.*

Still, I worried. An ocean, sure. But a river? Would it be sacrilegious to release ashes into the water?

Later that day, our tour guide pointed to a fire in the distance. "It's a cremation," she explained. "Sometimes, when we can't make it to the ocean, we release the ashes into the river instead." Her words were a Divine confirmation answering the question I hadn't voiced.

On the final day of my yoga retreat, our group visited a sacred water temple for a *melukat* purification ceremony, a cleansing of the soul. I stepped into the warm water, where five large fountains poured before me. They seemed to glow gold, each one representing a member of my family. As I moved from fountain to fountain, words echoed through me: *forgive and be free.* With each cleansing I felt the waters washing away generations of shame, resentments, and perfectionism.

When I reached the fountain that felt like my dad's, the air grew thick with love and the words shifted: *allow and receive.*

I bowed my head under the water, and the truth rose through me like a current: *There is only love. All the rest is illusion.*

The words didn't feel like mine alone. They felt like a message for all of us: *to forgive, to be free, to allow, to receive.* This is Connection—to feel your natural spirit again, alive and free, and to sense that same living pulse within you and all around you.

That evening, my mom and I descended seventy stone steps to a hidden waterfall carved with moss covered statues of gods and guardians etched into the rock. The whole place was ours. A dragonfly circled us, the same spirit animal that had appeared the week my dad passed. Together, with tears and tender words, we placed my dad's ashes in a beautiful flower offering and let them drift downstream.

As we turned to leave, I glanced at my watch: 5:55 p.m., the same time I had noticed the Hunter Moon the night he died.

Climbing back up the steps, a moss-covered carving stopped me: Rama and Sita, hand in hand, devotion etched in stone. I whispered to my mom, "Dad loved you like this," pointing to the carving. And then I thought: *this is devotion, not only to another, but to yourself. Devotion is honoring and living as your truest, freest self.*

Back in the present, Hunter's voice pulled me out of my reverie. "Look, Mommy, the snow is sparkling like crystals!" Children see magic everywhere. The sun had turned the mountain into a million diamonds.

We are like those diamonds, but we forget our brilliance. What if we slowed down enough to notice the sparkle and magic already within and around us?

Not long ago, I was drowning in exhaustion and disconnection, unsure of who I was becoming as a mother. Now, I was seeing the sparkle again. That's the gift of connection: when we forgive, allow, listen inward, and return to the heart's prayer, we receive the magic that's been here all along. We remember who we are.

> *Devotion is honoring and living as your truest, freest self.*

And what if you trusted that you, too, are already shining? That your worth isn't something to earn, but something you already are?

Our soul knows the way. When we open enough to notice, life reveals the magic that has been here all along.

The sparkle was never missing. We just have to remember how to see it.

The Gift

Connection is alignment with your truest self. Intention sets your compass. Attention walks the path. Embodiment lets you feel it in your bones. And surrender opens your hands to magic.

The gift of connection is this homecoming: alignment with your truest, freest, most authentic self. When you feel it in your heart, you realize you don't have to fix yourself or be anything other than who you already are. You don't have to do more, prove more, earn more, or be more. You are already enough. You are already worthy.

How do I know? Because you're here. Out of all the infinite possibilities, the Divine Source of Creation chose *you* to be on this planet, in this moment, with your unique story and gifts. Your existence is the evidence of your worth.

Your journey is to uncover your light and share it. Not by becoming someone else, but by becoming more of who you already are. And when you're in alignment with your true self, life flows through you and to you. The Itty Bitty Shitty Committee quiets down. You stop striving for worth and start living from it. It is a forever journey of knowing yourself deeper.

Joy is the gift you receive from a deep connection to your true self. It shifts you from resistance to receptivity, from forcing to flowing. From that place, everything—love, creativity, dreams meets you with more ease. Joy becomes the light you shine, and everyone around you feels it.

This connection always begins with love. To love ourselves is to remember that we are made of love. Everything, from our highest joys to our deepest heartaches, is wrapped in love. Love is the thread beneath it all. We come from love, we are love, we return to love.

Even when we feel alone, the word itself reveals a deeper truth: "alone" spelled out reads "all one." When you return to your true self—whole, free, and worthy—you remember what fear made you forget: **you belong. You are part of everything. You are *all one* with life.**

The more you embrace this truth, the more life unfolds in ways that feel divinely orchestrated, because they are. Life meets you at the frequency you embody. When you align with love, gratitude, and truth, life rises to meet you there. You're guided by synchronicities, nudged by intuition, and held by a presence greater than yourself. Trust, listen, soften, and let the pulse of life guide you forward.

Your worthiness isn't something you have to earn, prove, or manifest. It is the pulse of life within you, steady as your breath, certain as your heartbeat. It has always been here, and it always will be.

This is the sacred journey. To remember and reclaim, again and again, what your soul has known all along:

You are already whole.

Already worthy.

Already loved.

Integration

The Practice: Create Your Spirit Space

Connection is alignment with your truest self. Intention sets your compass. Attention walks the path. Embodiment lets you feel it in your bones. And surrender opens your hands to grace.

To bring this alive in your daily life, create a **Spirit Space** (a box, a jar, or a journal) that becomes a home for the moments that nurture your spirit.

Each day, place one small reminder inside. It might be:

- a moment of gratitude that made you pause
- a whisper of truth from your heart
- a synchronicity that felt like a Divine nudge
- something that sparked joy, peace, or aliveness
- a dream or idea that feels like a seed wanting to bloom

These are not just notes. They are evidence of who you are when you're connected to your spark, your intuition, your truth. Over time, your *Spirit Space* becomes a well of remembrance. On the days you forget your brilliance, open it and remember: Your spirit is always guiding you home.

Reflection

- What does my spirit long for and what simple action, thought, or shift would nurture that longing today?
- If I trusted my inner wisdom more than the Itty Bitty Shitty Committee, what dream or desire within my heart would I allow myself to follow?
- When do I feel most connected to my truest, freest self, and how can I invite more of that into my life?

Sahasrara Chakra

Embracing Spiritual Connection

The seventh chakra, *Sahasrara*, the crown chakra, rests at the top of the head and is the gateway to spiritual connection. Represented by the color violet, this chakra is where we open to the Divine Source and to the quiet wisdom beyond the mind. It's the place where we remember we are part of something greater than our thoughts, our roles, or our circumstances. We are woven into the infinite rhythm of life itself.

When this chakra is open, even for a moment, we feel a sense of oneness: connected to ourselves, to others, and to a Presence moving through everything. The mind loosens its grip, the inner critic softens, and we sense the deeper current beneath thought. When the crown chakra is out of balance, we may feel restless, anxious, caught in overthinking, unable to sleep, or disconnected from our bodies and from the magic woven into ordinary moments.

To bring this chakra into balance, nurture your connection to your true self and spirit. Connection, the final self-love tool, is not something you force; it's something you allow. When you quiet the mind, loosen control, and make space to listen inward, the crown begins to open. Like the thousand-petaled lotus that symbolizes the crown chakra, your spirit is always unfolding, petal by petal, into its own brilliance. Tending this connection invites you to open again and again, returning to the divine light, flow, and wholeness that have always been yours.

Mantra

I AM LOVE.
I AM WHOLE.
I AM CONNECTED.

CHAPTER 8

HOMECOMING

Remembering All That You Already Are

*"You are the hero of your own story. The privilege of
a lifetime is being who you are."*

—JOSEPH CAMPBELL

Two years after my dad's passing, Jake and I were blessed with another miracle, a baby boy, due on April 1st, my parents' anniversary. Life has a way of aligning moments with meaning, doesn't it? At 41, I'd been told my chances of conceiving again were slim, and if I did, it would be what the doctors so kindly call a "geriatric pregnancy." (Whoever came up with that term, I'd love to have a word!)

When my water broke at 39 weeks, I curled up on my bed with Hunter, listening to my hypnobirthing meditation. She rubbed her little hand across my belly, breathing with me. Soon, I was submerged in the warm water at the birth center tub, my body contracting, Jake behind me, steady as ever, washing my back with each surge.

Birth is raw and primal. It strips you down and calls you into potent presence. My labor was not the curated kind you see on YouTube. No lace bra, no perfectly made-up mom, no "just three pushes and baby's here" story. Nope. I was a full-on lumberjack in labor, growling and grunting with guttural sounds rising from a deep, ancient place within me.

And yet, even in the roar and bearing down, there was awareness—like meditation, where you become the observer and the participant all at once—both inside the experience and witnessing it at the same time. I watched as my body and baby worked together in divine union. Each contraction whispered, *You're closer. Keep going.* And in that gap between fierce effort and sacred stillness, I glimpsed the truth of life itself.

After an hour of primal sounds and deep pushes, my fingertips brushed against the silk-like moss of my baby's hair. "He's here!" I cried to the midwives, hand steady on his emerging head. Inside, I whispered again and again, *You and me, little one. You and me.*

And then, the miracle. His head emerged while his tiny fingers and toes still moved inside me. Part of him was out, part still within. A threshold. Two worlds, held in one body.

With one final roar, his body spiraled out of mine and into my hands. I pulled his fragile, slippery form to my chest, sobbing, "We did it! We did it!" Jake's tears mingled with mine as the room shifted from chaos to holy hush. The setting sun streamed through the window, painting the room in shades of lilac and rose, as if creation itself had gathered to witness his arrival.

We named him Bodhi, which in Sanskrit means "to awaken or reach enlightenment." Kind of a big name for such a little guy. But isn't that what life asks of all of us: to awaken to the beauty of Life itself?

Because that's what his birth was for me—not just a baby's first breath, but an awakening.

You see, enlightenment doesn't only happen on a meditation cushion in some mountain cave. Awakening happens right here, in this moment, in the mess and miracle of being human.

Awakening is being present to the magic of life. Slowing down enough to be in awe of simply being alive. Then we can see that everything is sacred.

Hunter's birth was raw and fierce; Bodhi's was intimate and transcendent. Both showed me the same truth: life is always inviting us to wake up to the sacred pulse within us and around us.

When I look into Bodhi's cobalt eyes, the same color as my dad's, I feel that truth. Joy and grief, love and loss, light and shadow—all of it woven together. And he reminds me daily: to be awake is to feel fully alive. Eyes fresh. Heart open. Present to the wonder that's been here all along.

Just as birth asks us to awaken to the miracles of life, so does life, again and again, inviting us home to our own worth and light.

And in that remembering, within you, too, a seed has always been waiting, quietly and patiently, to break open and bloom.

The Seed Within You

Whenever I feel stuck, I look to nature to remind me how to let go, nurture what is growing, and receive what is ready to unfold. Mother Earth is the wisest teacher. A seed doesn't need to know what it will become. It simply surrenders to its own becoming. It cracks open, pushes through the darkness, and reaches for the light of what it was always meant to be.

Mother Earth never rushes, yet she is always on time. She trusts the unfolding. And so can we.

Like a seed planted in darkness, you were born to grow toward the light and become it. When old stories and familiar fears take over, the **5 C's,** your self-love tools gently clear the way so your natural radiance can emerge.

Through **Consciousness**, you learn to recognize the voice of the Itty Bitty Shitty Committee and return to your true self, meeting the moment as it is, and seeing clearly what's actually true. From this awareness, you remember your power: when you're in consciousness, you're in choice.

You've practiced **Care** by tending to your inner child with tenderness and devotion, offering her the love she's always deserved. Through that care, you remember your worth, not as something *earned*, but as something *inherent*.

With **Compassion**, you've welcomed the parts of yourself that were once judged, hidden, or silenced. You've restored the broken roots by offering belonging where there was once shame. Compassion brings you back into wholeness.

And when fear tempts you to retreat back underground, you leaned into **Curiosity**, the willingness to stay open, to wonder, and to trust that there is more unfolding than what you can see.

Through **Connection**, you've remembered the truth of who you are, aligned with your authentic spirit and to the same light that lives in all things. This connection grounds you, guides you, and reminds you that you are never separate from the source of your becoming.

And here's the miracle: it isn't that the seed becomes an oak. The miracle is that the oak was already written inside the seed all along. And the same is true for you. Your worth, your light, your wholeness are waiting to be remembered and reclaimed. The 5 C's don't make you into something new; they simply help you return to who you've always been.

The Spiral of Remembering

Life will never be free of challenges, heartache, or disappointment. The Itty Bitty Shitty Committee doesn't vanish just because you've learned new tools. But as you practice the 5 C's, the storms lose their grip. You return to your true self more quickly.

With practice, presence and love become how you live. In quiet, ordinary moments, you choose again. To listen inward, to soften, to stay connected to what is true. Even seasons of fear or uncertainty become sacred invitations to remember who you are. Loving presence becomes your anchor.

Seen this way, life stops feeling like something you need to fix or perfect and begins to feel like a spiral of releasing what is false so you can remember and reclaim your truest, freest self.

Self-love is a verb, not a noun or a destination. It is a way of being.

This spiral carries you through contraction and expansion, through what cracks you open and draws you deeper into your truth. Each turn is a sacred invitation to know your depth.

Every time you feel deeply, every time you grow, you spiral inward and outward remembering who you already are. And each time you meet yourself and your life with loving presence, you come home to a deeper part of yourself.

You begin to feel life pulsing through you. And when you remember you too are part of that pulse, you live with more ease, more freedom, more sovereignty. Joy and sorrow, light and dark are not opposites. They are the weave of your sacred journey.

> *This is awakening: living in devotion to who you truly are and the sacredness of your own life.*

Honor how far you've come and the strength it has taken to be here now. Each step forward is also a step deeper into your soul.

The false self searches for certainty. The soul trusts the evolution in Divine timing.

This is awakening: living in devotion to who you truly are and the sacredness of your own life.

Your Sacred Journey Home

I hope that sharing my heart and story with you moves you to lean into your own story and live it in full recognition of your worth. Life is always speaking to you, inviting you to know yourself more deeply and listen inward to your inner wisdom.

While life's seasons aren't always easy, some even gutting, they carve you open, revealing the light within you, waiting to be remembered.

And what if your soul chose this human experience with this body and this life, so it could feel the full spectrum of being human? The heartbreak and the joy. The grief and the wonder. The ordinary days and the moments that take your breath away.

The gift is this: You get to feel it *all*. To be here. To be human. To walk this complex and beautiful journey of life.

Life's journey isn't just about finding your way through the dark. It's also about allowing yourself to savor the light. The joy, the ease, the moments that make you feel alive. Your challenges awaken you, yes, but so do your blessings. You are meant to experience all of it.

Our invitation is to see the sacred in everything—the mundane, and the miraculous.

I share this not as someone who has arrived, but as someone still unfolding, still on the spiral path, walking alongside you.

One truth I know is this: you are worthy. You always were. You don't have to prove, perfect, or perform to earn that truth. Your life itself is sacred.

The love, the freedom, and the sovereignty you've been seeking have always lived within you. There is nothing more you need to become. Only more of yourself to remember.

You are the path.

This devotional journey of remembering and reclaiming all that you are unfolds over a lifetime.

And the beautiful thing is,

a lifetime is what you have.

IN DEEP GRATITUDE

As I pause at the end of this journey, my heart fills with gratitude for all the people, seen and unseen, who helped bring this book into being. I also hold deep gratitude for you, the reader, who found your way here. Thank you for choosing this book. Thank you for offering your time, your attention, and your open heart. I believe that the way you tend to your spirit, the way you speak to yourself, and the way you remember your worth sends a ripple far beyond you. My hope is that what you've received here touches not only your life, but the lives of those you love. If this book has reached even one soul, and that soul carries its wisdom forward, it has fulfilled its purpose. *I wrote this book for you.*

This book has lived many lives. It took more than a decade to write, unwrite, and rewrite through different seasons, versions, and initiations. It truly takes a village to bring a book into the world, and I am deeply grateful to everyone who supported me directly through reading and editing, and indirectly through friendship, love, and life itself.

Jake, thank you for being my rock and my mirror. Thank you for helping me meet my shadows with honesty and my light with courage. Thank you for believing in me, in my gifts, and for encouraging me to share this work with the world.

To my children, Hunter and Bodhi, I love your courage, your authenticity, and your tenderness. You show me every day what it looks like to live in truth. You are my greatest teachers.

Deep gratitude to Saqib Arshad for your patience and meticulous care in shaping the interior of this book, and to Anze Ban Virant of ABV Atelier Design for your beautiful cover. You both helped bring this dream to life.

To my book writing coach, Megan Febuary, thank you for believing in this book when I couldn't yet see it clearly myself. Your encouragement helped me release an earlier version so I could reclaim my own voice. That act of trust changed the trajectory of this book, and of me.

I am deeply grateful for the editorial brilliance of Vesela Simic. Your ability to bring structure and clarity to my thoughts helped translate intuition into language and vision into form. This book is stronger because of your steady guidance.

To my friends and beta readers: Angela, Connie, Heidi, Jake, Jenn H., Jill, Mark, McKenna, Sarah C., Sarah M., Sarah F., Shradha, Steffie and Yazmina. Thank you for reading with such care. Your thoughtful feedback, insights, and encouragement helped shape this book in real and meaningful ways. I am grateful not only for what you offered to these pages, but for the time and heart you gave to this long process.

To Courtney and Amanda, thank you for walking with this book across a decade. You both read it multiple times, offering thoughtful insights, deep suggestions, and honest reflections that made a profound and direct impact on this work. Thank you for your friendship and for the depth you bring, not only to this book, but to my life.

To my *Founding Reader Circle*, thank you for reading an early version of this book and helping carry its message into the world. I know how full your lives are, and I am deeply grateful you made space for these pages. Your generosity to share this work creates a ripple of sacred remembrance, helping others remember their wholeness, their worth, and the truth that they already belong to themselves. The world needs more of you!

To the teachers who guided me deeply on my own self-love journey: Jana Wilson, Jennifer Prugh, Scott Feinberg, Kate Murphy, Sahara Rose, and Devi Ma. Each of you helped me listen more closely, trust more fully, and embody what I now share.

To my Mom, thank you for your unwavering support throughout this journey. Your love, encouragement, and the many ways you showed up made it possible for me to complete this book. I love you always.

To my Dad, thank you for encouraging me to write and for working with me into the quiet hours of the morning. Though this book is not the version we created together, I hear your voice every day, and I feel your support woven through this work. Thank you for walking with me still.

To my students and the communities I've had the honor of serving. Thank you for walking this path with me. Your willingness to show up, to practice, and to reflect these teachings back in your own lives shaped me as much as it shaped this work. You reminded me again and again why this book wanted to be written.

And to my dearest friends (you know who you are), who walked beside me as this book took shape through soulful conversations, encouragement, collaboration, and belief in me and this work. Thank you and I love you! Your support and love helped carry this book into the world.

And finally, thank you, Life, for the highs and the lows, the heartbreaks and the awakenings. Thank you for the invitations to shed what is false so what is true can be revealed.

Life is not linear, but a spiral, an ever-unfolding journey of remembering who we truly are.

It is an honor to be on this path.
It is an honor to remember.

ABOUT THE AUTHOR

Audrey Sutton Mills is a self-love teacher and intuitive guide who helps women remember their divine feminine power and return to their truest selves: worthy, whole, free, and sovereign.

With over fifteen years of lived experience and professional training, Audrey blends mindfulness, embodiment, spirituality, and practical self-love tools into a deeply human approach to healing. Her work is rooted in compassion, meeting the whole self with presence, tenderness, and truth. She helps women soften self-judgment, move through inner blocks, and reconnect with their innate worth, wisdom, and divine light that have always been within them.

Audrey's teachings are shaped by her own life experiences, including loss, motherhood, and seasons of deep transformation that asked her to listen inward and live more aligned. She believes the answers we seek already live within us. Through her work, she guides women to see themselves more clearly through love, trust their inner knowing, and live in deeper alignment with their soul's rhythm and purpose.

In addition to her writing, Audrey offers one-on-one private sessions, group programs, and transformational experiences and retreats around the world. She lives in the Pacific Northwest with her family and continues to walk this path of remembering alongside her students...one breath, one choice, one return at a time.

To learn more or work with Audrey, visit **AudreySuttonMills.com.**